Puerto Rican Espiritismo

Religion and Psychotherapy

Jose Morales Dorta

Second Revised Edition

The author's clarification note:

This research project was done during the first half of the decade of 1970. At the time, New York City demographic composition was, in some ways, different from 2013 population make up. Soon after World War II there was a massive migration from Puerto Rico to U.S.A. New York City became the promise land for hundreds of thousands of Puerto Ricans. We became the second largest minority in the big Apple. We encountered myriad problems other migrants had overcome before us with relatively ease. During the last three decades of the XIX and early XX century migration to the big Apple was from Eastern Europe joining other Caucasian earlier Europeans. Puerto Rican migration, on the other hand, was composed of European, Indians and African ancestry. Besides ethnicity, Puerto Rican migrant brought with him a rich Spanish culture and language.

He wanted to maintain and cultivate his identity as an American of Spanish cultural tradition. Consequently, he encountered the issues we addressed during the following research project. In order to move forward, Puerto Ricans made use of a religious practice he had at home, Espiritismo. At the time, Puerto Ricans were considered the Spanish speaking community of New York City. Later on, during the last two decades of the XX century, Dominican and Mexican moved in to the City in large numbers. They were followed by Central and South Americans presenting similar issues as earlier Puerto Ricans. We can say that Espiritismo and Pentecostal churches were significant influences in maintaining Puerto Rican culture, language and self-identity as an American citizen. Likewise, Mexicans with their rich cultural and religious tradition centered on around Virgin Guadalupe have strengthened New York City Spanish speaking community.

Contents

The Puerto Rican & Latin American Mental Health Patient.   5

Espiritismo and Protestant Churches as Mental Health Alternatives.   10

A Search for a Puerto Rican Religion: *Espiritismo* .   14

Origin *of Espiritismo* by Puerto Rican Spiritualists   22

The Marginal Puerto Rican (Historical Components)   27

An *Espiritismo* Seance   40

Case Presentation   66

Prayers and Herbs   72

Research Survey on Psychiatric Patients   83

Epilogue   90

CHAPTER 1

The Puerto Rican & Latin American Mental Health Patient

The problem of the dropout from mental health clinics and family service agencies has received considerable attention and concern from researchers and clinicians in recent years. In mental health clinics, recent studies have shown that up to 65 percent of the patients dropped out before treatment was completed.[1]

The seriousness of the dropout problems and its effects and complications in the community can be best understood if we realize that the 65 percent who chose to discontinue treatment were both disposed and motivated enough to come for the initial interviews. The group that sought psychiatric help and decided to discontinue treatment had enough strength to undergo the initial intake interview and possibly, after weeks of waiting, a psychiatric diagnosis, which was in turn followed up by a therapist assignment and treatment. (This is not to imply that this procedure is adapted by all mental health clinics.) A study on referrals to an adult psychiatric outpatient clinic revealed that, in general, patients were not seen in therapy for more than five office visits.[2]

The community becomes vulnerable to all types of unpredictable behavior because of the non -motivated, un-sophisticated, mentally and emotionally impaired, clinically-shy individual never gets to see a mental health practitioner. Individuals coming from low social-economic groups with both, multiple mental and behavioral problems, low motivation to seek adequate help are in the forefront of suicidal and homicidal attempts and death. This is the same individual exhibiting bizarre behavior with potential imminent violent behavior towards self and others.

These studies not only alert us about the high casualty rate (drop-out) during the treatment process but also, the need to develop more effective approaches and techniques in order to reach out and offer treatment to persons in need of mental health care.

A high incidence of drug addiction, suicide attempts, general apathy, and despair permeates the life of the poor of New York City. Our urban poor not only make more suicide attempts but also are more severely ill on admission to a hospital and have more previous hospitalizations than other groups living in suburban areas.[3] In New York City, the urban poor consists almost entirely of Latin Americans, Afro Americans and recent illegal migrants from around the world. Although no statistics seem to be available at present, the dropout rate from mental health facilities is probably much higher in the Latin American community than in any other ethnic group. Many factors can be discerned in this problem: racism, language barrier, cultural differences and discrimination, alienation from the mainstream of society, etc. In addition, traditional psychiatry has limited its therapeutic techniques to the middle-class American population whose life styles are more structured and open to cognitive-oriented therapy. Witness the lack of initiative in training community-minded people who have leadership qualities and concern for the health care of their compatriots. A system of referral networks and mental health care systems is virtually unknown in the Latin American community. If, for the sake of comparison, we consider the rate of dropouts for the Latin American students in the New York City school system, which by their twelfth year of schooling, is "80% compared to 40% for Blacks and 28% for Anglos,"[4] we might have a better idea of the current crisis in the delivery of mental health services to the Puerto Rican and Latin American community. Following the above statistics and assuming that Puerto Rican, Dominican, Mexican parents discontinue mental health services in proportion to the school dropout rate of their children, the number of Puerto Rican, Dominican and Mexican mental health casualties is twice the number of blacks and approximately three times more than Caucasian patients.

The Puerto Rican family places a high premium on the education of its children. While the children are small and the parents can still exert their authority and supervise them, the child is conditioned to attend school. Puerto Rican parents expect the school to provide for their shortcomings and limitations, as the school is considered the child's second home, *su segunda casa.* Thus, the parent naively accepts without malice both the school principal's and the teachers' advice on her child's education and behavior. There is no need to point out here the incredible gap between the parent's expectation of the school's role and the child's hard reality.

In the field of mental health, not only are Puerto Rican parents less knowledgeable, but the resources available, if any, rarely reach them. When the Puerto Rican comes to the psychiatric clinic, not only he is suspicious, but he also, finds himself face to face with someone who does not understand him. It is most probably that the therapist (psychiatrist, social worker, or psychologist) is an English-speaking person. In that case, an interpreter may be sought. The trust and confidence in the therapist has to be shared with a stranger who might himself become embarrassed translating and asking sensitive and personal questions. The number of Puerto Rican professionals in the field of mental health is probably not greater than those in the school system working as principals, assistant principals, guidance counselors, and teachers. "Each professional category is less than one per-cent of totals."[5]

In New York City over a quarter of a million (or roughly 25 percent) of the total school population is composed of children of Puerto Rican descent, and a study released by the census bureau revealed that 72 percent of all Puerto Rican families use Spanish as their main language. After twenty five years of massive migration of Puerto Ricans to New York City, the board of education still continues to ignore the needs of 25 percent of the entire school population. Puerto Rican professionals in the school system make up less than 1 percent of the total. Perhaps it is appropriate to indicate

7

here that, until a couple of years ago. Puerto Rican teachers with excellent qualifications and extensive experience, holding degrees from Puerto Rican and New York City universities, were not even allowed to call themselves teachers in the New York City school system. They were called (or arc still called) auxiliary substitute teachers, later upgraded to auxiliary teachers, "helping the Puerto Rican parent." No wonder the estimated dropout or "pushout" rate for Puerto Rican students has been put as high as 85 percent.

The casualty rate for Puerto Rican patients in mental health clinics shouldn't be expected to be any lower than that of the school dropout. As in the classroom, the Puerto Rican patient at a clinic office is treated (taught) by an English- speaking therapist with a theoretical background totally alien to the patient's culture. As in schools, communication (the language barrier) separates them. The patient who is unable to express his needs and problems and the therapist who is correspondingly unable to apply his professional armamentarium both soon become frustrated, exhausted, and disgusted. The patient feels he cannot win over the therapist, and the therapist may retaliate by stating that the patient is "unmotivated and unreachable."

A Case Presentation

Dona Juanita is a thirty-eight-year-old mother of five children, whose ages range from twelve to twenty years old. She was referred to the mental health clinic after a medical doctor told her that there is nothing physically wrong with her. Her second oldest son has been suspended from school, and the youngest child, a girl, comes home crying because other girls pick on her. She also learned last week that she was *"volviendose loca"* (becoming mad). She is then asked by the therapist to tell him her problems. In anger and despair she replies that she has told her problems to too many people already. She tells the intake person that she is ill from ner "nerves." The therapist insists on "probing" Dona Juanita's *past* life and history. Dona Juanita, looking at the therapist's wristwatch, communicates to her that she has to go because her children are coming home from school and she has to prepare dinner for them. As the therapist tries to "collect" more data for his "professional impression," Dona Juanita also tells him that on Thursday she has to report to the welfare center, meaning she is overwhelmed by problems.

Her daughter, who is sitting next to her, says: "Mom, remember that Carlos has a clinic appointment for tomorrow." The therapist, unaware of Doña Margarita's message to him continues to question her for more.

Dona Juanita jumps up and cries out: *"Ay Dios mío, que me voy a hacer yo"* ("Oh Lord, w hat am I going to do with myself?") She stands up and rushes to the door.

This case illustrates the problems alluded to in the preceding pages. Dona Juanita comes for help, *here and now.* She wants visible, tangible, and direct services. She is requesting concrete assistance helping her resolve her children's problems.

The therapist, on the other hand, is doing what is traditionally expected of him: to probe the patient's mind and feelings in order to be able to write an impression or diagnosis on her. Meanwhile, Dona Juanita's low frustration tolerance continues to increase, and she walks out of the clinic feeling she is a "helpless" case. She becomes a dropout patient and will probably seek out understanding neighbors and relatives for help. A Spiritism center or store front church would, most likely, be her next stop for help.

NOTES

'Social Work. 13. No. 3 (July, 1968). 48.
'Ibid.
•Social Work. V No. 2 (April 1970). p.39

Edwardo Seda Bonilla. "A Second Look at Cultural pluralism." paper read at Brotherhood in Action. May 1472.

'Richard Greenspan, "Analysis of Puerto Rican and Black Employment in N.Y.C. Schools" 1970, unpublished paper.

J. W. Kobrick, "The Compelling Case for Bilingual Education," *Saturday Review* (April 2, 1972)

Chapter II

Espiritismo and Pentecostal churches as mental Health alternatives

Traditionally a very religious people, early Puerto Rican settlers in New York City found themselves without a church to worship the Lord. Historically of the Catholic faith, the poor, unskilled, and "brown" Puerto Rican felt that the Irish- and Italian-dominated church was not a place for him to pray and worship God. The language barrier, the visibility of his skin color, and his extreme sensitivity on account of the discriminating practices of the white majority discouraged him from attending church.

Institutional religion is too far removed, rigid, and dogmatic to gain the trust and confidence of the poor. The constant daily need for survival, the need to act out fears, anxieties, and everyday problems are overwhelming. To go to church and sit silently for an hour is too demanding for the poor man to endure. He needs to talk, to tell his problems to someone who will listen and empathize. He feels that telling "God" is not enough. God knows he is poor and carries his cross. Many have found this support outside the Catholic and Protestant churches in Spanish-speaking churches of different denominations which have established themselves separately and apart from the traditional English-speaking churches. This has often been interpreted as a response to the Puerto Rican dropout or rather, "pushout" from institutional religions.

The Catholic Church made a small gesture to provide for her "alien" children and heal the gap. Spanish instruction was recommended for priests in churches with large Puerto Rican and Latin American membership. Priests were brought in from Spain and other Latin American countries. (We should note that the church in Puerto Rico was under the Archdiocese of New York until recently.) During the past four years the church has intensified its efforts to establish deeper and closer ties with Spanish speaking communities in the country in general.

Not only has the number of Spanish-speaking priests increased, but some of its clergy have become deeply involved with the community in the resolution of problems other than spiritual. Workshops and seminars are being held in Puerto Rico for those in the church who want to better serve and understand Puerto Rican and other Spanish speaking persons. Despite these efforts, however, the Catholic Church remains removed and distant from the Puerto Rican community, with a few exceptions where the priest has taken an unusual position. On those few occasions the priest has left the pulpit of his church to fight for and help his parishioners resolve their "worldly" problems. Another recent exception among the Catholic priesthood is the liberal group which is a promising force. Ethnic self-identity and self confidence in its cultural and language strength.

Puerto Ricans soon learned that it was not too difficult to get a certificate of incorporation and establish a church outside the traditional institution. They felt the benefits of the small group, which afforded them security and a sense of belonging.

There are two religious groups which are strongly identified with the Puerto Rican community in New York City—*Espiritismo* (spiritism) and the Pentecostal sect. They have spread and nourished in our community with unexcelled strength, speed, and zealousness. The relationship among its members is one of warmth, love,

11

support, mutual understanding togetherness, and companionship. Almost every member of these respective sects is known to each other in a very familiar fashion, and the church relationship is carried home. This is, perhaps, the most outstanding characteristic attributed to the growth of local churches. It is as if the friendship and trust gained in the church is carried home making their friendship even stronger. Each church member contributes with concrete help: money, food, clothing, and, often, shelter. They share information among themselves about housing, employment, welfare, schools, etc. Each one has a responsibility toward the other. The leader, whether he is a president of a Spiritism center or a pastor from a Pentecostal church, is a person who lives in the same community. Although he might not be well versed in theology or have a college degree, he is very close to his congregation. His church, as well as his home, is open to the parishioner.

Usually coming from the same socioeconomic and cultural background as his parishioners, the pastor offers "a living proof of one's ability to advance by faith and hard- work."[1] In both the espiritismo and Pentecostal groups, the leader is a respected person in the community. He serves his community spiritually, morally and physically. Problems of every nature and origin are discussed in each "seance." The pastor helps his parishioner with problems of a spiritual nature as well as with problems relating to the person's physical self. Therefore, money, housing, school, health, and family problems are all considered part of his responsibilities. The Pentecostal church, with a membership of approximately 20,000, has the largest number of Spanish-speaking people.

The Pentecostal congregation has a registered charter in Albany, thus enabling it to open storefront churches. These churches are recognized by a large and highly visible sign in front of the "store."

The total membership in an individual Pentecostal church is often small. They usually have meetings three times a week. The small size of the group and the close relationship among members facilitates mutual understanding and cooperation. Each one expects the other to behave according to the church rules at all times. Their social, as well as their spiritual life, is centered on the church. They do not tend to wander outside their group. It is said that "Pentecostals post the greatest challenge to both Catholic and traditional Protestant movements in attracting Puerto Ricans."[2] This seems to be substantiated by a recent study of the National Council of Churches. It shows that substantial numerical gains for the last few years were made by churches with a Pentecostal orientation or a vigorous conversion drive.[3]

The other cohesive, firmly knitted group of persons known as *espiritistas* is hardly known outside their congregation. They hold their meetings in the privacy of their homes. Unlike Pentecostals, they rarely have storefront churches, nor do they preach on the streets. They do not attempt to persuade one into their belief through the teachings of the Gospel. Unlike most Western devotee religious, the Holy Bible is not their *holy book.* However, the Bible is used as a source of reference to document their beliefs. Although their teachings and practices can be traced back to time immemorial, their religious theory was elaborated in the second half of the nineteenth century by a Frenchman. His books are to the *espiritistas* what the Bible is to Christians.

In a way, *espiritistas* feel they are a gifted and chosen people. They feel they are gifted in that they can communicate with the dead. Or, as some of them have put it, "the spiritual world chooses us to communicate to the world around us". This communication might be with their loved ones who have died recently or with people who lived thousands of years ago. *Espiritistas* believe that if one is chosen by God to disseminate their cult, sooner or later, one will end up an *espiritista* through different tests or challenges by God. They claim power to cure illnesses and to expel evil influences in individuals. Many emotionally disturbed people find refuge among them.

A fully developed *espiritista* believer becomes a medium. Mediums believe not only that they are possessed by spirits and communicate with the world beyond, but that they can also foresee a person's future. In many ways, the job of a medium is similar to that of a therapist in a mental health clinic. Many people consult a medium for their problems before they see a medical doctor. Often, though, doctor and medium are seen simultaneously by the same person. There is a great difference during the communication between them. With the medical doctor, their meeting is professional, objective and usually cold while the spiritism meeting is warm, trusting and within the family network.

In the following chapters, you will learn about *espiritismo* and its development in Puerto Rican society.

NOTES

[1] Wagenheim, Kal, *Puerto Rico: A Profile* (New York: Praeger, 1971), p. 163. 2-Wakefield, Don, *Island in the City: The World of Spanish Harlem* (Boston: Houghton Mifflin, 1959), p. 76. 3- "Conservative Church Slow Growth," *New York Times.* April 15, 1973.

Chapter III

A Search for a Puerto Rican religion: Espiritismo

Over seventy years ago, a man dressed in the cloth of God, said, "Puerto Rico is a Catholic country without a religion."[1] These are the words of a man who saw Puerto Ricans on the island for the first time. He was part of an invading force to "liberate" the islanders from the Spaniards. A contemporary Puerto Rican writer said, "Puerto Ricans are a religious people in search of a religion."[2] Both the American chaplain and the islander are saying the same thing. If being a Catholic means to love,

14

care, and protect one another (*Samaritan*), to practice the hospitality of the good Samaritan, to be humble, to love and care for the elders, to love the Lord above all things on earth, then this is a religious people. The hospitality of the Puerto Rican and the intense feeling and respect for the things of God is known by those who have visited the island. This spirit of brotherhood and love for another is carried over to New York City. A religious and good Samaritan, a Puerto Rican cabbie risks his life "to save a drunken derelict."' The cab's passenger, a state investigation commissioner, apparently impressed by this demonstration of love for one's neighbor, felt the incident was worthwhile being reported to the newspapers.

Yes, Puerto Ricans are a religious people, as observed by the chaplain, the writer, as practiced by a taxicab driver, andas felt by many who have been helped by an individual Puerto Rican.

But they also have a native religion. It is a religion practiced in every home, but rarely discussed outside. It is *espiritismo*. *Espiritismo,* or spiritism, is frowned upon and often the object of attack by the organized church. Despite church censure and attack, it has remained the underground religion of the Puerto Rican both on the island and on the mainland. Although the upper class tends to say that its *espiritismo* is different from that of the lower class in that it is "scientific and experimental,"[4] the belief in spiritism is an integral part of the Puerto Rican life and culture. Religions in general tend to appeal to the poor, and it is in this segment of our society that *spiritism* is strong and widely practiced.

But *espiritismo* among Puerto Ricans is more than a religion, especially to the poor. They feel it serves not only the spiritual nature of man, but also the body and the psyche. It relates, explains, and treats daily problems. It is a psycho-zoma spiritual doctrine. It purports to explain and provide for the spiritual man, but has also developed techniques to cleanse the body from "problems and imperfections."

Espiritismo, besides being a religious cult, is a folk

system of psychotherapy used to deal with many illnesses, especially those that have been treated for a long time unsuccessfully by orthodox methods. A note of clarification seems appropriate here. During a visit to the medical doctor the patient expects him or her to use his medical knowledge, training and technological advances to diagnose and cure his illness with a magic pill. The patient is a passive recipient during the medical visit. In a spiritism séance the patient is an active participant during the diagnosis and treatment process. It involves not only 100 billion neurons in the brain establishing new circuits and pathways otherwise dormant, but the soul, if you wish, provoking and supporting new mental images of hope and accomplishment to bring about emotional and physical changes. The patient seems to be in charge of his own treatment, nature healing process will do the rest. When you are wounded the clinician will clean up your wound, but leave you alone so your body will do the rest. When you are sick with a virus, your clinician will ask you to rest and let your body defense system, basically, B and T cells to identify and take care of your invaders. During a spiritism séance the patient is mobilizing psychic, emotional and physical forces to overcome problems around us. Besides all the above, they always call for the power of God too help them discover solutions to their problems. It is widely practiced to thank messenger of God, and God himself for all the blessings they receive. A spiritism séance is very demanding and places the patient or believer at   the center of stage.

Before describing *spiritism* and its practice among the Puerto Rican poor in New York City, I would like to trace *spiritism* as explained by its believers.

Espiritismo as practiced by Puerto Ricans on the island and in New York City is based primarily on the writings of a Frenchman known by the pseudonym of Allan Kardec. He is a native of Lyons, France. He died in 1869. Hypnotism and its allied "sciences" were at their peak at the time. However, it was from Hydesville, New York, in the 1850s with the Fox family that spiritism, or communication with the dead, became a "great discovery." Shows or demonstrations of spiritual communication by mediums (persons who were able to communicate with the dead) were held in the United States and in great cities of Europe. For a while, it not only developed into good business, but was secretly practiced by known personalities and socialites. Kardec's writings were well received in Latin American countries and very enthusiastically in Puerto Rico. "Twenty- one specialized periodicals emanating from seven urban centers over a period of 75 years do seem to testify to the popularity of spiritism in Puerto Rico."[5] The total population of the island at the turn of the century was about one million persons. Illiteracy was very high—so naturally, it was not the poor person who was reading these papers. During the second half of the XIX century upper class Puerto Ricans went to Spain, France, and to a lesser degree, Germany, to get their professional degree. The point in question is that they must have known the spiritism theory of their colleague, Allan Kardec. These professionals, medical doctors and lawyers, brought from Europe Kardec`s theory. Paris and Vienna in Austria were the greatest center of learning where the most gifted gather to show their talents.

The books by Kardec found in every espiritismo *center are* The Book of the Mediums, The Book of the Spirits, The New Testament according to Spiritism. *There are other smaller pamphlets and booklets, including* Colección de Oraciones Selectas *by Dr. Alexes Carrel.*

In the more sophisticated groups or centers, one might find, along with Kardec's books, the writings of Amalia Domingo Soler. She was a Spanish spiritualist who wrote bitterly about the Catholic Church. Books of Elipha Levi, Edward Schure, Annie Besant, and Mme H. P. Blavasky often make up part of the *espiritista's* library.

Just recently (late 1970), a "new" influence has come to the *espiritismo* movement. This "new" E*spiritismo* comes from South American migrants to New York City. In Argentina there seems to be a well-organized E*spiritismo* cult with chapters throughout other Latin American countries. The scientific approach is strongly emphasized in the Argentine movement. It claims to work in cooperation with professionals in education, medicine, law, etc.

Kardec teaches that, along with our material-corporeal world, there is another, invisible world. This invisible world is the home of the spirits. The spirits, like their world, are invisible. In every person there is a soul or spirit which is in a process of "evolution" or progress throughout the "plane" earth. Each individual person must allow his/her spirit to express itself and develop its celestial faculties. The spirits are not omniscient, though they can appear anywhere, at any time. Some of these "developed" spirits are very wise and knowledgeable, but there are also ignorant, mischievous, destructive and confusing spirits. Kardec teaches that we must get in touch with the spirit in us and allow it to guide our thoughts and life. The most important thing to do is to listen to the spiritual guide existing within you. This guide (no gender) is responsible for guiding you through a myriad of problems and sacrifices you need to go through for self-fulfillment and accomplishment.

As the person becomes aware of the spirit within him, he is also providing for communication with spirits of the invisible world. It is a dual process. It is stated that, as the rational man learns to communicate with the spirit in him, he is at the same time opening a door and a line of communication with the world of spirits. It seems that an invisible world populated by spirits exists alongside the material or physical world.

It leads us to believe that, just as there are people in the physical world who want to communicate with the "world beyond," there are also spirits in the invisible world who want to communicate with humans in the physical world. The person who can serve as an intermediary between men and spirits from the "world beyond" is called a medium.

Kardec's book of the mediums teaches different levels and grades of spiritual development. Each spirit incarnated or disincarnated must go through this law of spiritual evolution to attain and fulfill its mission. The spirit achieves different levels and grades through *pruebas.* It is a kind of a task that a spirit, disincarnated or incarnated in a person, must perform to pass to another level. It is through the medium that the person learns about his *prueba.* However, since there are many kinds of mediums, the nature of the *prueba* is not very clear. A highly developed medium might interpret and describe a *prueba* differently from a selfish or jealous medium. Not to add to the confusion, but it is also true that a spirit communicating to a medium might be in a low level of evolution.

The mediumship process becomes more complicated as we learn that the incarnated spirit has relationships with spirits in the "world beyond." An angel from the invisible world of the spirits always follows and serves as a protector to each incarnated spirit. There are other spirits of lesser importance that accompany the incarnated spirit. This lesser spirit is called *guia,* or guide. When these lesser spirits come together, they are called *protecciones,* or protectors.

A person who is able to see spirits is called a medium with visual faculties. Those w ho can hear and "feel vibrations" are called auditory and sensorial mediums. There are somnambulist and healing mediums, etc. Psychology has multiple specializations, and so is biology, astronomy, medicine, etc., not that different from spiritism practice.

Since the practice of *Espiritismo* is mostly concentrated in the poor and uneducated Puerto Rican population in New York City, the interpretation of Kardec's religious cult varies not only from center to center but also from one medium to another in the same center. When you listen to 2013 television evangelist you may have the same problem. The doctrine itself teaches different levels of progress in each spirit, both disincarnated and incarnated. Therefore, it provides in itself for different interpretations and opinions. However, where the leadership is strong and effective, there is togetherness and enthusiasm. Although each medium may have a different interpretation, they do not tend to discredit each other. They emphasize spiritual development stages.

It must be brought to mind that the *espiritismo* religious doctrine is not different from Christian teaching: Thou shall love thy Lord above all things.
Thou shall love thy neighbor as thyself.
Do unto others as . . .

These are basic in their religious practice. The New Testament, according to E*spiritismo* interpretation, is the "teaching" book used at the beginning of every *reunion,* or spiritual meeting. An interesting aspect of *espiritismo* and its implications in mental health is the "here and now." Progress is measured in terms of what you do for yourself and others *now. T*he thing is to "do," and to act in the present time. It is not a verbal and intellectual journey into your past life and experience, it is what you feel and experience during the séance. If it demands from you to cry, laugh, and jump or address someone in the audience, you must do it. You must be honest about yourself and trust mediums sitting at the table. It may require a person to do something for another person or for himself. When something may look suspicious, it is taken over by the entire medium ship for evaluation. It may be called peer review or supervision.

A person may be asked to help another person in need or visiting ill people in hospitals, as these actions are helpful toward spiritual progress. He might have to read from the Bible as well as practice some rituals at home. Rubbing ointment and lotions on his body is also done. *Espiritismo` s* reliance upon Christian teachings of repentance, confession, prayer, and appeals to God for help have a strong healing force in the person's mind. Among the classifications of mediums, there is one called "healing medium," or *curandero.* He is well versed in the healing process and knowledgeable in the use of herbs. This *curandero* medium is very busy in the Puerto Rican community.

His office, usually a *botanica,* an herb store, or a dimly lighted room in his apartment, is crowded with people seven days a week. This *curandero* medium seems to be the Puerto Rican counterpart to the Mexican *curandero* of which anthropologist William Madsen writes as quoted by Robert Edgerton, *"Curanderos* have effected true recovery in several cases of mental illness in Mexican-American ailments."[6] Madsen explains that the success of Mexican *curandero* is due to the psychiatrists' ignorance of the value conflicts and social stresses of the Mexican. More of this will be discussed in following chapters.

Notes

1-Kal, Wagenhein, *Puerto Rico: A Profile* (New York: Praeger, 1971), p. 159.

2- Ibid.

3-New York Daily News, *April 12, 1973.*

[4]*The Puerto Rican Spiritualist as a Psychiatrist* Rogler & Hollingshed, Abstract, p. 5. Paper read before the Section on the Sociology of Medicine at the Annual meeting at the American Sociological Association held in New York City in 1960. 'Joseph Bram, *Spirits. Mediums and Believers in Contemporary Puerto Rico* 343.

The New York Academy of Sciences, Ser. II, 20, No. 4 (February, 1958).

• Robert B. Edgerton et al, in "Curanderismo in the Metropolis," *American Journal of Psychotherapy.* 24, No. 1, (January, 1970), p. 125.

21

CHAPTER IV
The Origin of Espiritismo by Puerto Rican spiritualists

To have a better understanding of *espiritismo* as practiced by New York City Puerto Ricans, the writer feels it necessary to illustrate the historical background as *espiritistas* see it. Every *espiritista* interviewed by the author admitted that Kardec's teaching is their main source of information. However, they insist that although Kardec consolidated and systematized the doctrine, *espiritismo* has existed for ages. *Espiritistas* make profuse quotations from the Bible to validate their contentions. Visions of old prophets such as Ezekiel, Isaiah, and Daniel were spiritual communications given by spirits of high level called guardian angels. According to *espiritistas,* the teachings of Christ fulfill and establish forever the existence of the invisible world of spirits. They accept Jesus as a fully developed spirit and the son of man in the process of becoming a son of God. Hebrew prophets are fully developed spirits serving as messenger for God. Moses and Christ are Hebrew's most prominent spiritual guides ever existed on planet earth.

When Jesus was asked by Pontius Pilate, "Art thou the King of the Jews?" Christ responded, "My Kingdom is not of this world." Jesus not only avoided limiting himself to any ethnic or national group but unequivocally established the existence of another world. In talking about resurrection, *espiritistas* often quote St. Paul: "Now if Christ is preached as risen from the dead, how do some among you say that there is no resurrection of the dead? But if there is no resurrection of the dead neither has Christ risen; and if Christ has not risen, vain then is our preaching, vain too is your faith."[2]

Those are the words of the apostle of the gentiles and which are frequently used by many *espiritistas.* Christ arose from the dead is interpreted to mean from the world of spirits and that Jesus alone had the power to make himself visible in both worlds. Likewise, Jesus' reference to "In my father's house there are many mansions"[1] is believed to be the different grades and levels of the spirit world. Each "mansion" houses "guardian angels" spiritual guides, protectors, spirits of trials *(pruebas),* etc.

Since the spirit has no death or birth but lives for all eternity, we must, then, love God in the spirit and not in the body, which is subject to decay. "God is spirit: And they that adore him must adore him in spirit and in truth."[4]
The truth is no other than Jesus Himself who comes from God, the Father. Espiritismo claims a long list of adepts throughout history. Among the most outstanding is Joan of Arc, who is considered an auditory medium, for she claimed that she heard voices from heaven, telling her what to do during her struggle against the British soldiers? Ignacius of Loyola, founder of the Jesuit movement, was another medium in the *espiritismo* cult. Loyola, a captain in the Spanigh army defending the city of Pamplona against French invaders, was wounded. While in bed, he heard voices telling him to lay down his sword and develop an army for the salvation of the faith. Then the Jesuit Order, like a spring of water, spread all over the world, propagating and defending the word of God.

Another world-renowned Sephardic Spaniard, Saint Theresa of Jesus, a mystic of the Catholic Church, is known by E*spiritismo* to be a highly developed medium. Saint Theresa said she was tormented by visions and celestial voices. She thought she was becoming mad, as she felt the presence of the Lord wherever she walked. Psychic experience has been attributed to many people, past and present. *Espiritismo* may claim Akhnaten, an Egyptian pharaoh, at the time of Moses, called "the world's first idealist,"[5] the first known medium. He is the first known king to lead his people to worship one God, an invisible God who manifested itself in the sun.

However, not in the past or in any faraway country, but here in America, *espiritismo* has a good number of proselytes. Ruth Montgomery in her book, *A Search for the Truth,* said that Thomas Edison was a spiritualist, and she further added: "Edison, perhaps with the help of spirit communication, brought us the electric light bulb, the phonograph, and other remarkable inventions." Edgar Cayce is called the "Sleeping Prophet of America," and his A.R.E. Foundation has thousands of members in its affiliated organizations throughout the United States. In a state of unconsciousness, his spirit (he called it entity) could search the body of interested individuals, diagnose the illness, and prescribe treatment and medicine, usually herbs and homemade remedies.

However, it is in Washington, D.C., that the world's best-known psychic, Jean Dixon, resides. Ruth Montgomery has given us an excellent account in her book on Jean Dixon's psychic power. Jean, like *espiritismo* followers, claims that she has heard voices from the world beyond and has had visions. Believers of *espiritismo* could cite innumerable instances of psychic experience or communication with the dead. But *espiritismo* as practiced by the poor seems to be more passionate and intense, with an overlay of their problems and sufferings. For them, the spiritual meeting *(reunion)* is not only an hour of prayer for the salvation of the spirit, but time to cleanse their body of physical afflictions.

It is not naive to say that the belief in spirits has no geographical or time limitations. Whether we call it *espiritismo,* psychic power, or E.S.P., it seems to have adepts from all layers of society. "Belief in the works of the spirits is by no means restricted among either Puerto Ricans of New York City or those on the island."' *Espiritismo* as explained by Kardec has many manifestations and may take various forms. Apparitions, visions, and healings are daily happenings. *The New York Times* (November 22, 1972) ran a page on an apparition at West Point, New York. There was a drawing of the apparition by a cadet who emphatically insisted that he saw the ghost.

The *New York Sunday News* (September 24, 1972) took

the time and money to run over three pages in the accounts of "The Miracle of Herman Wijns." It is the story of a ten-year- old boy from Belgium during the German occupation. While playing with other children, Herman, "hearing a voice calling him," went to look, and had a mortal accident. The medical doctor could not sign the death certificate because "the body is dead but not the soul." Experts came from different parts of the world to see "the child whose soul lives." A stranger, known to no one, and who did not identify himself, was able to help Herman depart to the "other world" and be buried. There is no doubt that many of us have heard of similar cases and stories and wonder why they continue to attract our attention.

The Spanish press carries frequent cases of this nature. Such stories are not limited to Spanish-speaking people, but occur all over the world. Whatever their nature is, the stories almost always come under the label of *Espiritismo or the world of the spirits.*

Temas, a widely read Spanish magazine in New York, Puerto Rico, Latin America, and Spain, dedicated two pages to a case history of "medium healing" in Italy (July, 1972). The medium, Signora Valente of Naples, doesn't hear voices nor see visions. The article says that the healer takes only cases referred by medical doctors. Her treatment is based on placing her fingers at specific parts of the body according to different ailments. Signora Valente does not attempt to explain the why, the what, and the how of her faculties, but doctors and the public do not stop from coming to her.

The world of the occult, of ghosts, mediums, clair-voyants, telepathists, etc., is fascinating, often confusing and complex, but so is the world of the teachings of Christ. Two thousand years after Christ crucifixion, very few dare to dispute an iota of His teachings, although we may not agree with all of teachings.

There are undoubtedly energies generated by the human mind of which we know virtually nothing. Research tells us that the average person uses only about 10 percent of his brain capacity although the brain is always busy doing her things. One hundred billions neurons added to about 850 billion glia cells in the brain with the potential of trillions of synapsis gives you the most powerful and sophisticated computer ever imagined. With such an unlimited use of our brain, one wonders why we become so defensive when dealing with the unknown. The scientific world of the nineteenth centuiy opened a new era for mankind, and the technology of the twentieth has opened avenues to new sources of energies. New discoveries, not in outer space, but in the human body are used to diagnose according to the colors[8] of an energy surrounding the body.

I would like to close this series of references on psychic experience with a statement from R. C. Johnson on psychical research: "With the recognition of new energies and new phenomena quite outside the scheme of physical law, pointing as they do away from material order, the climate of opinion created should be more sympathetic and open to consider the data of revelation."[g]

The above-mentioned quotations have been made with the purpose of showing you that belief in the world of spirits, or world of the dead, as some may call it, is not restricted to Puerto Ricans and can be traced to time immemorial. However, this should not be interpreted as either condemning or supporting *espiritismo*. I have just attempted to show you some of the sources that believers of *espiritismo* draw from, to justify their cult.

NOTES

'John 18:33. 36.
'Cor. 15:12, 13, 14.
'John 14:2.
'John 4:24.
'Silverberg Roberts, *Akhnaten, The Rebel Pharaoh* (New York: Chilton Books, 1964).
"Ruth Montgomery, *A Search for the Truth,* (New York: Bantam Books, 1969), p. 231.
' Don Wakefield, *Island in the City: The World of Spanish Harlem* (Boston: Houghton Mifflin, 1959), p. 60.

' Sheila Ostrander and Lynn Schroeder. *Psychic Discoveries Behind the Iron Curtain,* (Englewood Cliffs, N.J.: Prentice Hall, Inc., 1970), p. 206. R. C. Johnson, *Psychical Research: Exploring the Supernatural,* (New York: Funk & Wagnalls, 1968), p. 170.

CHAPTER V

The Marginal Puerto Rican (Historical components)

During Spanish colonial days, Puerto Rico was called by Spaniards their most faithful "daughter." Perhaps the Puerto Rican current political status as the Commonwealth of Puerto Rico can be best explained as another "marginal" position of the Puerto Ricans. A very outstanding Puerto Rican, Rene Marques, in *El Puertorriqueño Dócil,* give us a good picture of the fragile personality of the Puerto Rican. It is important that we become aware of these feelings and attitudes of the Puerto Rican to be able to understand the development, strength, and growth of *espiritismo* practice. Did Puerto Ricans adopt *espiritismo* as a protective practice against the established church? Is it a marginal position giving them some sort of security? Or is it a cult which developed from different religious and ethnic groups beliefs on the island?

To further understand the need for "secrecy of worship." we must trace it to Puerto Rican religious history and to ethnic composition. At the time of the Spanish colonization of Puerto Rico (sixteenth century), the island was inhabited mostly by a peaceful Indian tribe called Tainos. A religious people, they believed in a supreme being called Yukiyu. They also believed in minor or lesser deities called "cemies." Protecting each village and each family there was a cemi. Imagine the power of this Puerto Rican god against earthquakes, hurricanes, nearby volcanic eruptions as well as assault by nearby aggressive tribes.Depending on each family, economic and social status, each one had a cemi carved in wood, clay, stone, or gold. This idol worship doesn't seem to be different from religious practices today in some Christian countries. It is most conspicuous with Catholics and Orthodox Christians whose homes and churches are well adorned with pictures and statues of many saints. Puerto Rican Indians, like Christians, believed in a protector god who dwelt in heaven. Like Christians, they also believed in a world beyond death that could be reached after death.[2] This religious practice of the Indian was abolished by the Catholic Church at the time of the colonization. Despite destruction of Indian deities and persecution of worshipers by the Spanish authorities, at home the Indian continued to worship his god and smaller deities. Hard labor, disease, death at the hands of the Spaniards, and exile greatly diminished the Indian population on the island. To compensate for the loss of the Indian population to work in the gold mines and in agriculture, African slaves were introduced on the island. The Africans brought with them their religion with its rituals and deities. But, like the Indian, the African slave had to be Christianized under the new church of the conqueror. One cannot but imagine that Indians and Africans alike continued to worship the gods of their ancestors in the privacy of their homes. This religious practice had to be conducted under strict secrecy because of the risk of being caught by the *hacendado,* or landlord, and severely punished.

This writer, in tracing the history of *espiritismo* in Puerto Rico, points out that the contribution of Indian religious practice at the time of colonization and the introduction of African religious beliefs through the slaves brought about the development of a native religion. It was not only the Indian and the black person who worshiped in an underground church in Puerto Rico. During the sixteenth- and seventeenth-century mysticism as practiced in Spain aroused suspiciousness and persecution by the Catholic Church. This was the time of the Reformation and the Inquisition. Great Spanish mystics like Ignatius of Loyola and Theresa of Avila suffered much hardship and persecution by ecclesiastical authorities. Like today's "mediums," these mystics claimed to see and hear celestial beings. Then, as today, the Catholic Church was very scornful of those who professed unorthodox religious beliefs. Having visions and holding conversations with Christ and the Virgin Mary was not a monopoly of a few Spaniards; it seems to have been a widespread practice. However, such claims have not only brought condemnation by the church, but it has exposed people to social criticism as well. You may be considered a lunatic or someone just seeking attention. As a result, the Spaniard who migrated to Puerto Rico had good reason to keep his mystical beliefs to himself lest he be subject to social criticism and religious scorn. But the population of Puerto Rico during the first two hundred and seventy years was extremely slow. The few gold mines on the island were soon exhausted, and newland and treasures in Mexico and South America made it difficult to attract colonizers to Puerto Rico.

A population census taken on around 1765 showed only 45.000 people in Puerto Rico. The first 300 years of colonization was a time of almost complete social and economic neglect. Spain had its vast empire extending from western United States to Argentina to take care of. There were much land and vast riches elsewhere. The island of Puerto Rico was of great interest and importance to Spain, but Puerto Ricans were not. San Juan, the capital, was made an impregnable fortress. Fortress El Morro stopped the invading armies of England, France, and Holland. The Spanish galleons, loaded with gold from the colonies, found comfort and security at the powerful walls and cannons of El Morro on the island. Huge treasures passed by Puerto Rico, but never stayed there. By the time Americans were saying "give me liberty or give me death," trying to break the yoke of colonialism, El Morro in San Juan, now fortified and greatly improved by the Spanish king, was an impregnable fortress that aided in the continuation of colonialism. At the end of the eighteenth century, Puerto Rico was a neglected and poor island, but with a strong military fort guarding Spain's vast colonial territories in America. It was also a time of great political and economic upheaval. The beginning of the nineteenth century brought many changes in the American continent.

The great movement of liberation that took place during the first two decades of the nineteenth century in the Spanish Empire in the Americas found very few echos among Puerto Ricans. Despite intense neglect and abuse by Spanish governors on the island, the political theme during the remainder of the nineteenth century and under Spanish rule in Puerto Rico was assimilation with continental Spain. It seems that the three hundred years of complete social and economic neglect of the population, reinforced by the presence of an invincible military compound, created a feeling of extreme dependence and castration in the Puerto Rican. There is the docile, fragile, submissive, obedient, and loyal Puerto Rican described by Spanish as well as by American critics. The fear of overpowering force has been used in many societies to create a docile and submissive population. Hostos, a very prominent Puerto Rican of the nineteenth century, called his own island the "lost paradise."[4] He says that despite all abuse and neglect, the island was restful, conforming, peaceful, loyal and gentle as if made of wax; the Puerto Rican adjusted to a new situation without a fight. In my opinion, that was an unfair statement. Puerto Ricans challenged and overcame many problems and threats. We will overcome never left their lips. Although basically a person on guard secondary to multiple invading forces to the island, he avoids confrontation and decides for a passive settlement or a noncooperative consent. *"Que sea lo que Dios quiera"* ("Be it what God wills") reflects his feeling of resignation and helplessness, but keeps his machete in case you do not understand him. Thus, a marginal, noncommitted attitude seems to have been the preferred choice for survival of the Puerto Rican, and it has survived 115 years of American dominance. That attitude may have helped Honorable Sonia Sotomayor get to the U.S.A. Supreme Court in Washington, Jose Acaba, our first astronaut, Admirals, Generals, scientists, Congressman and local politician in mainland cities. In business we find Puerto Rican in the highest echelon of corporate

America.

Puerto Rico at the beginning of the nineteenth century was a conservative and Catholic as well as military stronghold. The United States, a Protestant country, moved into Louisiana, and many French and Spanish Catholics, fearful of American Protestantism, went to Puerto Rico. South Americans from Colombia and Venezuela, at the defeat of the Spanish army by Bolivar, left for Puerto Rico. Also Spanish from the Dominican Republic, fearing black Haitians who had conquered their country, took refuge on the most loyal colony Spain ever had, Puerto Rico. Thus, Puerto Rico became a haven for ultraconservatives, Catholics of all nationalities, and sympathizers of Spain. With Protestantism strong in that growing country of the north, the United States, and revolutionary movements to the south, Puerto Rico reinforced its dependency on its protective church. It need not be said that anything that did not conform to Catholic dogma and teachings was taboo. Politically, Puerto Rico was governed by military men who not only abused their power but cared the least for the island's political, economic, and educational growth. However, the nineteenth century is called the "golden age" of Puerto Rico. The children of wealthy Puerto Ricans went to Spain and France for their education. During the second half of the century, there was political activity on the island as well as great suppression and governmental abuse. Most of the political leaders had to go underground or into exile.

In religious practice, the situation could not have been different, and we can assume that many Puerto Ricans continued to practice their religious belief behind closed doors. We must also bear in mind that the Catholic Church, one of which was located in the main plaza in each town, was far removed from the native population. It was a church of worship and not a way of life. The priest, a non-Puerto Rican, not only supported the political system on the island, but could not meet the natives' needs. Besides, poor peasants had neither the time nor the means to attend church services in a city that was miles away. Therefore, two religious practices developed under the name of one church. Most Puerto Ricans called themselves Catholics whether they ever visited the church and practiced *espiritismo* or not.) Those living in towns where the church was located attended regular Sunday services. These persons, although professed Catholics and attending church, would practice *espiritismo* among relatives and friends. There was also, besides the peasant, the rural dweller who felt his form of religion (*espiritismo*) was more realistic and pure. He talked to someone who spoke his own language and not Latin. He related with people whom he had contact with almost every day of the week. Although *espiritismo* was widely practiced on the island during Spanish rule, it had to be practiced *callado,* in secret, as the Catholic could not permit another form of religious practice regardless of the church's tolerance or perhaps indifference toward the religious needs of the population. Thus, the statement by an American chaplain who said that Puerto Rico was a Catholic country without a religion could be justified because he could not see nor understand Puerto Rican reality. The chaplain failed to see that there was a religion— *espiritismo. Espiritismo,* as a way of life and as a religion, was replacing the decaying and indifferent Catholic Church. Wagenheim, in his book about Puerto Rico, says: "Puerto Rico Catholicism is hardly orthodox; it is often mixed with personalistic worship, spiritism and superstition."[5] The Puerto Rican Catholic clergy has always come from outside. It has been an "alien" clergy. During Spanish rule, the clergy was composed of Spaniards; under American rule, the clergy has been either Irish or Italian. It took the Pope almost five hundred years to name a Puerto Rican cardinal. This came about after many demands from Puerto Rican Catholics and the threat of an ever growing Protestant movement in the rural and poor population of the island.

One wonders if *espiritismo* as an underground religious movement helped to develop and strengthen the separatist and independent movement on the island during the second half of the nineteenth century. According to Antonio S. Pedreira, as quoted by Joseph Bram, *espiritismo* papers were published and widely read as early as 1880. We must bear in mind that, at the time, 80 percent of the population could not read or write. We may assume that, as *espiritismo* changed from a mouth-to-mouth religion to one with the printed page, it became known by the Puerto Rican educated man as "scientific" *Espiritismo.*

Despite the conquerors' drive for assimilation during both Spanish and American rule of the island, the Puerto Rican developed and kept his own personality. Perhaps because of guilt and feelings of inadequacy, based on colonial humiliation and rejection, the islander developed his own self behind closed doors. San Juan looks just like any other American city, but inside the buildings there is a Puerto Rican who looks, feels, thinks, and worships unlike other Americans. Avoiding open confrontation and fearful of self- destruction, he has settled for a compromise, allowing modern living, housing, cars, TV sets, dress, and the like. However, the Puerto Rican continues to be attached to and defend his own identity despite the great intlux of Americanism. *"Yo soy jibaro donde quiera que voy"* ("I am Puerto Rican wherever I go") is heard in New York as well as in San Juan.

The Puerto Rican is very sensitive toward rejection by Americans, but he also seems to fear assimilation and in-corporation into American life. He takes pride in his historical past and points to Hispanic culture and accomplishments with great satisfaction. However, there seems to be confusion as to what he can call a Puerto Rican culture. It seems that the best of his cultural tradition is Spanish, although lately it has been influenced by Americans. It may be argued that the Puerto Rican reliance upon his Hispanic background and preference for a marginal position is a self-defensive mechanism aimed at protecting his fragile personality. This statement may lead to confusion because Puerto Ricans have proven otherwise during most adverse situations.

As indicated earlier, the most common and frequent form *of espiritismo* is practiced behind closed doors in private homes or apartments. Puerto Ricans seem to be aware that this form of religious belief is not shared by their fellow Americans. They feel Americans look at it as a primitive and uncivilized type of tribal worship. The Puerto Rican, being visibly different in his brown skin color, speaking a different language, and proclaiming a different culture, may be tolerated in this multiple racial and cultural city. He has accepted this somewhat unclear position. (To date, 2013, you find people in New York City practicing religions never heard of before). However, to practice openly an "alien" religion is something that Puerto Ricans are neither willing nor prepared to do. Puerto Ricans seem to opt for a marginal position as long as they maintain their own identity. If assimilation in the mainstream of American life is not their desired goal, neither do they seem to want to establish themselves separate and apart from American society. We can appreciate this position by their political status on the Island. Puerto Ricans continue to remain under American rule economically and politically despite almost 500 years of colonialism. They seem to be content to control just the local affairs of the island. However, their fellow Puerto Ricans on the mainland compensate for the lack of representation in Congress.

In the following chapter you will be taken to an *espiritismo* center. You will learn about the incense, the working table, candles, prayers, music, the names of the spirits, etc.
However, I must inform you that the practice of *espiritismo* differs from one center to another. Although their religious doctrine is basically the same as Kardec wrote it, the manner in which different mediums present themselves is interesting and fascinating.

NOTES
[1] Kal Wugenheim. *Puerto Rico; A Profile* (New York: Praeger, 1971), p. 40.
2- Department of Education, *Paginas de Nuestra Historia,* (San Juan, Puerto Rico: Estado Libre Asociado, Depto. de Instrucion, 1959), p. 20.
3-Jose L. Vivas, *Historia de Puerto Rico* (New York: Las Americas Publishing Co., 1962). p. 120.

4 Lidio Cruz Monclova, *Historia de Puerto Rico.* (San Juan, Puerto Rico: Editorial Universitaria, 1957), II, p. 432.
5-Kal Wagenheim, *Puerto Rico: A Profile,* p. 160.

CHAPTER VI
The Espiritismo Center

In New York City there are at least two kinds of *centros-espiritista.* There is the storefront type of *centro* which resembles that of Pentecostal churches. Usually, the medium or would-be president begins his church in his apartment with a handful of believers. As the word of his *facultades,* faculties, is spread around the neighborhood, the number of his converts begins to increase. Most always, among those coming for *consultas*, or consultations, the medium finds that they are in the process of *desarrollando facultades,* developing spiritual faculties. After a while, the medium's apartment is too small to accommodate all those who come for "spiritual help." So, the time has come for the medium to suggest to those who are "developing spiritual faculties" that a formal *centro* must be established. They form a board, with the medium as president, and secure legal services for a certificate of incorporation. As soon as they are chartered by the state of New York, they begin their business as any other religious group. The size of the *centro* usually averages 15 by 30 feet. There is no outside sign indicating that it is an *espiritismo* center. It is unlike the *botanica,* or healers, who flamboyantly display their services and merchandise with large signs. The *botanica* attendant and the *curandero* somehow expect to be paid for their services, although they do not profess it publicly.

The *centro* holds its *reunión,* or spiritism meeting, during the evening. Usually it begins at approximately 8:00 P.M. and extends to 11:00 P.M. on Tuesdays and Fridays. On Sundays, the meeting begins around 2:00 P.M. It is most crowded on Friday; people don't have to get up early the next morning to go to work. As believers in *espiritismo* come to the *centro,* they take their places intuitively, as if told beforehand where to sit. They know that chairs around the table are restricted to mediums that *trabajan causas,* meaning a medium who can work out somebody else's problems. Another term usually given for this type of medium is *pasar los espiritus,* one who allows a spirit to manifest itself through that person. After the "working medium" comes the person with *facultades, meaning* faculties, but he cannot *pasar espíritu.* This medium may have visions, hear voices, feel "spiritual vibrations" in his body, etc., but cannot allow a spirit to possess or enter his/ her body. This group is often called *desarrollando facultades, meaning the one* in a stage of developing spiritual faculties. They also know where to sit. They take places close to the table and near the working mediums.

There is also another type of *espiritista* who knows where to sit. This is the person who does not seem to show any symptom of emotional problems. He is not a medium, nor does he have any special faculties. He believes in E*spiritismo,* he has faith in it and hopes some day he can develop spiritual *facultades.* He usually sits next to the group developing faculties. It is worth noting here that being a medium is a status symbol among the Puerto Rican poor. There are two other individuals w ho can be easily spotted at the *centro.* One is the troubled, confused, and emotionally disturbed person; the other, the person who comes there out of curiosity. Of these two, the latter most always sits in the wrong place. He often takes the place of a medium and has to be asked by the president to move to another seat if he does not work *causas.*

The emotionally troubled one takes the outside chair. He looks somewhat scared and becomes suspicious of anyone's looks or remarks. He is quiet but attentive to what is taking place in the *centro.* He hardly talks to anyone and doesn't move from his chair. Obviously, he is the most anxious of all members present. He hopes the meeting or seance will soon begin, although his heart palpitations might be heard two seats away. He feels he is in need of help and wants *espiritismo* help, but he is afraid the mediums will expose all his problems and wrongdoings to the audience. He is not only afraid that the

36

medium will also force him to tell in public all the bad things he has done, but that a spirit may overtake him and make him roll over on thfe floor. Everyone who has decided to attend an *espiritismo* meeting has had some orientation as to how it works and is aware that these things do occur. He goes there with some expectations, but also misconceptions and fears. The *espiritismo centro* is the place to communicate with the other world, the world of the departed ones. That alone makes many people have fearful anticipation.

In the center of the meeting room is a table. Usually, it is two dining tables placed together, seating comfortably from six to eight mediums. There must be enough space between each chair, so the medium can move comfortably. This arrangement might change from one center to another, but the table is centrally located so everybody in the room is able to see what is happening on the table. Likewise, the mediums seated at the table will have access to everyone. In most *centros,* the table is covered with a white cloth. However, there are also *centros* with red or dark blue cloths on their tables. Some places do not use any cloth at all. On the table you will see at least two jars of water. These jars of water are used by mediums to cleanse out people's *causas,* or spiritual fluids. These spiritual fluids, or currents, as they are often called, are symbolically taken with the medium's hand and placed in the water jars. This process of cleansing oneself of spiritual "fluids" and "currents" is also known as *despojo. Despojo* can be done by a medium if she is working through somebody's *causa.* Or it can also be done by the person himself. The most orthodox spiritism séance are done with a white table cloth covering the table. This is known as Espiritismo of Mesa Blanca.

In fact, a kind of self-*despojo* is required before you leave the *centro* at the end of the *reunión.* The jar of water is also used as a "crystal ball" by some mediums. They claim to see their visions in the water jar. The water in the jar is usually blessed by the president. Next to the water jar are the books used for reading and prayers. As mentioned earlier, the main books used are those of Kardec and the Holy Bible. The crucifix has an outstanding place on the table. There is also paper and pencil for the "writing mediums." They write things seen, heard, or felt, so when it is time for them to speak, they don't forget them. Also on the table you may find "Florida water." It has a very pleasant smell and is said to allow for the spirits to come to the *centro*. The contents are 75 percent alcohol and several herbs. Symbolically, it "scares away bad spiritual influences and establishes a collective communion with God." This marks the beginning of a séance. Complete silence is mandatory. Small crying children are better left at home.

The burning of incense is another part of the ritual in a *centro* as it is in many established churches, but in *espiritismo* it seems more pronounced. Incense comes in all colors, shapes, and odors. Rani, a very popular Hindu incense made in Chicago, has a fragrant and refreshing smell, and is used by many *espiritistas*, both at home and at the *centro*. It comes in cones and sticks. Wisteria, cinnamon, jasmine, and sandalwood are some of the flavors burned at the *centro*.

Candles, like incense and Florida water, are the third indispensable instrument of all mediumship practice. The dim light of a candle seems to create a favorable atmosphere for people, so their minds are concentrated on one thought: God. Looking straight at the light of a candle is recommended by many mystics down through the ages the world over. This practice facilitates concentration and meditation. Some historian claim that candle burning for meditation purpose comes to us from Central Asia through Persia, Babylon and Greece.

Música espiritual, or music especially composed for *espiritistas,* is always played at the *centro*. Unlike traditional religious music, it is fast and high-pitched. Some mediums demand a specific record or song for them to work through a spirit, or *causa. Otherwise, silence is the rule.*

Behind the center's table are shelves fixed to the wall. Plastic figures of saints are set on these shelves. Saint Barbara, Lazarus, and Saint Anthony seem to have preference at all *centros;* also small statues of Indians are a very common sight at the *centro*. A statue of Jesus Christ has an outstanding place on the shelves.

The other type of *centro* that the writer was referring to is the private spiritual meeting, or *reunión,* that is held in the medium's home or apartment. This is the most numerous and popular, but also the most difficult to get into.

The number of private seances held in the city's Puerto Rican community would almost be impossible to enumerate. They are held in secrecy and in the privacy of the home. Very often, *espiritismo* meetings are held across the street at one's neighbor's home; but one would never know. A mysterious "cloud" seems to cover the place where the seances are held. The mediums and members who meet in a private home tend to have a very close relationship among them. It appears that their social life is determined by the *espiritismo* seance. They seem to develop a very trusting relationship so as to help each other economically; they go to parties together and exchange presents among them. The president or principal medium always remains and maintains the dominant role in the group, therefore keeping an eye on the group's behavior. He or she may not present himself as friendly and as outgoing as the rest of the members.

The attendance at these private seances is limited to a small number. The physical facilities and the secret nature of the meetings do not provide for a big gathering. Since they are held in private homes, one needs an invitation to attend. This invitation usually comes from a "host medium"; his approval is always sought. Those invited ones who come for help are few in number and receive individual, intensive care and attention. Often, one will find a group of five or six mediums working on only one person. The "patient" not only has the support of the group, but he is also convinced that he can rely upon each member for help. Telephone numbers and addresses are exchanged between "patient" and mediums, thus reinforcing their relationship and trust in each other. After the patient's problem, or *causa,* has been worked out, he/she is requested to read prayers from one of Kardec's books. He/she is often referred to the *botanica* for herbs and incense. The patient is motivated to come back for the next session and report about his health.

Chapter VII
An Espiritismo Séance

Few of these small private groups go out in public as an incorporated institution because of the requirements of a charter in Albany, the financial burden, fees charged by a lawyer, etc. This is besides the time required to work out their own *causas* and develop their own spiritual faculties into mediumship.Now that you have learned about the spiritpsm meetings and about the different components of a *centro,* I will take you to an *espiritismo* seance.

It is a Friday evening. Time, 7:30 P.M.; location, Sunset Park, Brooklyn. Slowly, you open the door and a very fragrant odor makes you begin to feel that you are going into some kind of trance, or perhaps into the unknown world of the dead. But most probably it is a cone of Hindu incense. As you take the second step inside, the *espiritista* music, the burning of candles, jars of water on the table, and a sizable collection of Indian heads, Arabs, and saints' statues surely do much to convince you that you are about to witness a communication with the spirits of the world beyond. Everybody comes quietly, sits down and waits for the president or authorized medium to announce that a séance is about to begin.

The *centro* president takes his "place," and the working mediums sit around the table. The light switch is turned off, and a dim light is left on the table. By this dim light mediums and the president read the prayers or biblical passages from one of Kardec's books. The music can hardly be heard now. There is complete silence among the members attending a séance. If you feel like scratching your face, you don't. You want to see and hear everything that goes on around you. The president calls for an opening prayer: *"Pudre Nuestro que estas en los cielos. . . ."* ("Our Father who art in heaven. . . . ") . Everybody in the room prays. The presidenthas commanded it, and everyone seems to be willing to follow him and cooperate. Many eyes are fixed on the president, and some on the mediums sitting around the table. The president seems to assume the expected role of absolute supremacy of the father; and the female mediums, the self-sacrificial role of the mother, a very dominant family value and role expectation of Puerto Rico and Latin American countries.[1] The magic "aura" and the fantasies of omnipotency attributed to the father figure (the president) is many times multiplied and strengthened by the person's belief that the president can communicate with a world unknown to him. The mystery behind all religions tends to place on its priests (the president) power not shared by other members of society. After the prayer is done, the president instructs one of the persons around the table to open the book of Kardec (the gospel according to *espiritismo*).

They usually spend from thirty to forty minutes reading from the gospel. These readings may need to be clarified or expounded on by further readings from other of Kardec's books or from the Bible. These readings are aimed not only at bringing about concentration and meditation, but about developing a sense of group cohesiveness and feelings of belonging. They are expecting something to happen to all of them, a religious inspiration or cure of their illness. Thomas Moore, as quoted by Samuel Z. Klausner says: "religious experience gives strength, conviction, and confidence, and has a mental hygiene value peculiarly its own."[2] For many Puerto Ricans, *espiritismo* is not only a religion, a form of worship, but also a therapeutic modality.

In most *centros de Espiritismo,* the president goes among everybody sprinkling them with *agua benedita* (Florida water). As the readings continue, the president emphasizes the seriousness of the session or seance. He calls for unity of thought and says, "It is between you and God." The readings may be complemented with passages from the Bible. Mediums sitting at the table may be called upon to explain to the group the meaning of what has been read on an *espiritismo* level. Often, comments from the audience are welcomed. If different points of view arise in the interpretation of the readings, the president always makes the last judgment. After the readings and interpretations are over, the books are closed and neatly placed on the table. The president stands up, and facing the picture of Jesus Christ, says: *"Este centro se abre para el bien y se cierra pura el mal"* ("The Centro is officially open for supreme goodness and closed for evil spirits"). With that pronouncement, the mediums are told to begin to receive communications with spirits. However, there is not a single uniform practice for *espiritismo.* And, the opening of the *sesión* may differ from *centro* to *centro.*

There are *centros* which open the *espiritual* session to spirits with the president holding hands with mediums around the table in solemn prayer. The prayer calls on God to allow good spirits to manifest themselves and give power to reject the evil ones. Some mediums and the president himself tie a handkerchief around his head and eyes. Blindfolded, they block out distractions and can concentrate better and allow spirits to come over them easier. It is emphasized over and over again that you are addressing God, therefore, honesty and trust is supreme during each séance.

Once the session is officially opened by the president, mediums begin to show that they are receiving f*luidos* or spiritual vibrations. This is marked by different facial changes, expressing pain or joy. The medium's body begins to tremble on the chair and is often followed by jerking bodily movements. A distant and whispering voice may be heard from a medium asking the "table," meaning, the other mediums around the table, permission to communicate or express himself. It means that a medium has been possessed by a spirit and wants to express himself/ herself through the medium. The president gives the OK to the spirit to communicate, by saying: "In the name of the Father, the Son, and the Holy Spirit you are welcome." Most communications from a spirit or medium begins with, "May our Heavenly Father's peace be with you." The president and other mediums may respond: "Amen." The communicating spirit continues to verbalize through the mediums. Without pointing out or calling anyone, the spirit may say: "Oh, dear sister, I have troubled you for many years. Oh, my dearest sister, forgive me. I have come here tonight, to this holy place to ask you to forgive me so 1 can leave this world of suffering for a place of heavenly peace." The spirit continues: "I am *un espíritu de existencias pasadas,* a spirit of past incarnation who torments you day and night. Oh, dear sister, I come from deep in the darkness where everything is cold. (The medium shakes as if she were feeling cold ness.) There is only darkness and suffering where I come from." Still without identifying himself / herself or indicating whom it refers to, the spirit continues talking: "I came here because there is light. How frightening is the darkness. I am thirsty, 1 am hungry. Please, give me a piece of bread." As the spirit asks for bread, the president, the mediums, and often everybody in the *centro* join in a prayer: "Our Heavenly Father, forgive our sins . . . Holy Father give us our daily bread." As the spirit talks, the medium may display many facial expressions and bodily movements. Her voice may change from a low whispering to a cry of joy and satisfaction. The president or one of the mediums may ask the "spirit" to identify the person she is referring to. The spirit decides not to reveal the person and continues to talk about the *causas,* or problems or sufferings, the spirit has placed on the person, and says: "1 place on you a severe pain in the stomach, and you cannot eat anything. 1 make you lie down on the bed and cry, but nobody can find anything wrong with you. I get you confused and disoriented. Sometimes you wish you could kill yourself because you feel very unhappy."

By this time, the president as well as the rest of the mediums at the séance has become impatient. This spirit is taking up too much time and doesn't address itself to anyone. Besides, there are other mediums that have begun to give signs that they have received vibrations from spirits who are waiting for the "green light." Once more, the president addresses the medium that has been possessed by the spirit and says, "Can you point your finger at the person on whom you have placed the *causas*?" The medium may make a vague gesture, and the president, facing the audience, calls on anyone who suffers from the problems or *causas* mentioned by the spirit. The attention of the group is focused on that spirit or medium. People begin to feel all kinds of problems and pains. These problems and pains tend to grow in intensity as the medium talks. The symptoms, or *causas,* described by the spirit are felt by a considerable number in the audience. They came not only for help because they were in pain, but because they want to believe in *espiritismo.* People want to cooperate and make themselves accessible to communication from the world of the spirits. Mediums as well as the general public, those who profess *espiritismo,* believe that if you do not cooperate and deny or reject the spirit's claim on you, it will slow down, *la obra,* the teaching of *espiritismo.* It will be harmful for the spirit and for the person who denies or rejects the spirit's "influences" over him.

As expected, there is more than one hand raised indicating he or she is the person the spirit refers to. However, the spirit most always picks the person at the command of the president. There are times when the president has helped the spirit find the person whom he has come with. This is done by the president's clarification of symptoms to the person. At times, the president may say that he, too, received vibrations from the spirit and that he knows the person with the *causas.* Besides, the president, because of his unique position and all the attributes and expectations placed on him by the audience, can easily manipulate the situation to his advantage.

Once the identity of the person has been established, the president directs that person to answer the spirit. If the spirit says, "I place on you a *causa* on the left side of your head every night before going to bed," the person is to say yes or no. In this way the person witnesses (*comprueba)* that the medium is telling the truth and that it is a spiritual communication. The person must limit himself to a yes or no answer. The president reminds the person to answer the spirit honestly and frankly. If he doesn't feel the pains as described by the spirit, that person must say so. Honesty in the presence of God is emphasized.

While the spirit is talking, the president, as well as other mediums at the table, pleads with the spirit to repent, to leave the tormented person alone. The spirit is told of the harm done and the suffering and pain that the spirit has inflicted on the *tormented one.* The spirit is told to make a self- examination and to realize that a spirit belongs to the world of the dead. The spirit is told to leave that "material" or physical body. The spirit is advised to recognize itself existing as a spirit, and that in so doing, his progress and development will be accelerated. If the spirit continues to harm and torment the person, the more ignorant and deeper into darkness he will get. The spirit is asked to see the light and find a heavenly place with the Lord Jesus Christ.

Espiritismo practice not only differs from one *centro* to another, but mediums have their own peculiar way of working with and addressing a spirit. During this time, a complicated and intense interrogation may develop between the spirit, the tormented person, and the mediums. The mediums may interrogate the spirit about its own identity, degree, or level of spiritual development, reasons for tormenting the person, and other *causas* or problems and pains felt by the mediums, etc. The tormented person is usually interrogated about his belief about *espiritismo.* He is asked whether she was aware of spiritual vibrations. He is often told how to recognize the "fluids," or vibrations, from the spirits.

The intensity of the interaction depends on the emotional makeup of the medium and the tormented one. As indicated earlier, some mediums are loud and emotional; others are very quiet and orderly. It also depends on the manner in which the spirit manifests itself. A vociferous, belligerent, rebellious, and uncompromising spirit may require the working or help of every medium at the *centro.* It may make the tormented person roll all over the floor, go into big rage, cry, laugh, pull at his hair, etc. While the spirit talks, he is told by mediums to repent. Mediums call on God and Christ to help the misguided and confused spirit. The spirit is asked to repent and to return to his world.

However, if the spirit doesn't begin to feel remorse and want to repent for his wrongdoing, a direct action by another medium may be called for. The president or a medium will hold the possessed medium by his/her hands, and, with an invocation to God and the medium protective guide, the spirit is ordered out of the possessed medium. In all the sessions that the writer has attended, the president and assistant mediums have always been able to drive away the evil spirit.

Now, let's take a more critical view of this first manifestation of spiritual experience just described. The possessed medium, through the spirit, verbalizes and acts out his problems and pains. The medium becomes the central focus of attention. He has unique powers or gifts not commonly shared or possessed by others at this meeting. It gives him some social status, recognition, and praise by others. At the same time, we can say that he is ventilating and projecting his own feelings.

However, if he is acting out her behavior by screaming, yelling, crying, jumping, etc., and projecting his feelings and thoughts, he is doing it with approval and support from the president and the mediums. He is not held responsible for his behavior while possessed by the spirit. If there is any blame, it is placed on the spirit. The medium is to freely allow the manifestation, and the exteriorization of his feelings and thoughts. He is to express visual and auditory communications from the spirit as well as bodily sensations or "vibrations." The tormented person is requested to be honest and sincere in reporting and checking out the spirits claims on him. The symptoms or *causas* presumably placed on the tormented one, even when remotely and vaguely remembered or felt are to be acknowledged by him. The medium as well as the tormented person is expected to open up to the spirit and avoid denials or other defensive mechanisms. It would only block and hinder spiritual progress and development.

While attending *espiritismo* sessions, the writer has compared this type of spiritual communication with a psychodrama session. The stage in psychodrama is the table in the *centro*. The director is the president. The auxiliary egos are the mediums around the table. The audience is the same for both. The subject, or patient, is the tormented one. In both psychodrama and *espiritismo,* there is a warmup period, and the

46

patient is expected to portray his own internal private world. The director, like the president, directs, analyzes, and treats the patient. Mediums, like auxiliary egos, can be extensions of both patient and therapist; of both president and the tormented one.

However, the patient in *espiritismo,* unlike in psychodrama, can be the tormented person as well as the "possessed medium." Both persons become the focus of attention. They are to express openly and without reservations their feelings, thoughts, and problems. In psychodrama the patient is subjected to intensive interrogation by the therapist and the audience. At *espiritismo* centers, intensive interrogation by the president and the mediums is done. The possessed medium can give vent to fantasies, inhibitions, suppressions, and otherwise unacceptable impulses without fear of condemnation. In fact, he/she is encouraged to do so. The anxious, tormented person is relieved of guilt as his feelings and thoughts are projected and displaced in neutral or external grounds. The spirit is blamed for the patient's problems. If the patient committed adultery, it is blamed on the spirit; thus, guilt is relieved. The patient is reminded by the mediums to keep in control of himself and not to allow the spirit to overcome him. He is advised to pray and is given remedies to expel the spirit. If the tormented person has hallucinations, it is blamed on the spirit. If there are sexual and aggressive impulses tormenting the person, they are also blamed on the spirit. These are *causas* brought on by the confused, misguided, and sinful spirit. This kind of acceptance and tolerance of abnormal behavior at *espiritismo* sessions provides for self-exposure with great freedom. As in psychodrama, the patient has to act freely, as things rise up in his mind. That is why "he has to be given freedom of expression, spontaneity."[3]

The possessed medium and the "tormented one" act freely with maximum freedom. There no restriction or criticism for behavior while under the influence or in the possession of spirits. Whatever comes to mind must be ver- balized. However, this is not to be interpreted that the patient or subject can go on and on acting out his behavior with the approval of the mediums. The patient, or subject, in *espiritismo* is expected to change and modify his behavior as his *causa* is worked out in the *centro*. The spirit in the possessed medium may be a very difficult one. This prompts the other mediums to come to the rescue and help the possessed medium to control and teach the spirit a lesson. This is done when the spirit doesn't leave the medium. At this time, there may be a show of power between mediums. They want to test their *facultades,* or spiritual progress.

Each spirit is departed from the medium with a prayer. Before the spirit leaves, the tormented person is given a *despojo.* The *despojo* may be that she swings her hands around his head. This is supposed to be done in good mental concentration, and hands must be swung fast. The whole body becomes involved in this movement, and at the end the person feels tired. It seems to be an excellent way to release tension. An auxiliary therapist or medium may help the tormented person with the swinging of the hands. The purpose of the *despojo* is to clean the person of the spirit's vibrations, or *fluidos. Despojos* may take different forms. They may be done by the patient himself or by a medium.

The medium other than the patient doing a *despojo* has to undergo some type of preparation. She/he must know how to do it, or she/he may carry with her/him some of the patient's *causas.* Often, the patient is asked to make three complete turns to the right and three to the left. This is followed by making the sign of the cross around the head, arms, and legs. There is a specific number of cross signs to each part of the body. While this is being done, the president demands complete silence and mental concentration. Everyone's mind is concentrated on God, praying and asking Him for help. No matter what your physical and emotional affliction are at the time, your concern is for the patient and you must be willing to do all you can to help him after the spirit has left and the patient or tormented person has been given a *despojo.* He/she may be requested to apply some remedies at home. Some remedies are herbs, teas, rubbing of the body with a special kind of ointment, bathing at home followed by a ritual, dedication of candles to saints and spirits, etc.

48

The president in a *centro,* unlike the therapist in a psychodrama, has at his disposal a set of reinforcers or remedies for the patient. The patient is given something concrete to take home and work with. And, unlike psychodrama, *espiritismo* has God, the church, and the Bible. It has a redeemer, Christ, whom the patient relies upon when he can't have the therapist. Thus, *espiritismo* becomes a therapy for the mind, body, and spirit.

A person, be he a medium or the president, usually has more than one guide, or *guia.* When two or more *guias espiritual* are known to the person, they are called *protecciones,* or protections. Naturally, the more protections a person has, the better off he is. These *protecciones* are also known as *cuadro espiritual,* or group of spirits. Within the *cuadro* there are spirits in different level of spiritual development and progress. They can work different *causas* and can restrain rebellious spirits. Most mediums often boast of their *cuadro* and their power. However, there is always a very close, protective, and wise *guia* or spirit with each medium besides the *cuadro.* This protective, omniscient, omnipresent, and omnipotent *guia* can be part of the *cuadro,* and often he is the leader. This superguide is always ready to defend the medium, and the medium is ready to indulge his demands. The writer feels he must emphasize that prayers, said either by individual members or collectively by mediums and audience, are an integral and very important part of *espiritismo* sessions. Prayers at the *centros* are the same as taught and practiced by the Catholic Church. A good portion of prayer is dedicated to the Virgin Mary. As in Catholicism, *espiritismo* devotees believe in the holiness and Immaculate Conception of the Virgin Mary, and also believe in most Catholic saints.

Mediums use prayer as their greatest protector and weapon against the wrongdoing of spirits. Elena Padilla, in her book *Up from Puerto Rico,* describing *espiritismo* belief among Puerto Ricans, says: "To counteract these powers (revengeful powers of spirits, ghosts and the devil), a person can pray to God, the Virgin and the Saints as well as to the spirits whose task it is to shield their wards from unhappiness and illness."[4]

49

Therefore, prayers are said throughout the session.

Espiritismo has many approaches for the subject who seeks help. The following is a description of the working out of a *causa* when all the mediums of the *centro* take part in *trabajar la causa,* or working the *causa.* Usually in this approach, the president or a respectful and well-known medium calls on a subject from the audience. He is told to stand up and come forward to the table. Unlike the first case presentation, which resembled psychodrama, in this approach, the tormented person or the patient is immediately identified. He is told that a *causa* has been placed on him by a spirit who wants to evolve to a higher level of spiritual progress. The president also identifies the spirit and tells the patient the reason for his *causa.* He also describes the spirit in its fullest detail. The spirit may indicate that he doesn't mean any harm, that he has seen the light and needs a few prayers and forgiveness from the patient. He might indicate that his intention has been good, that he wanted to bring the patient into *espiritismo.* There are numerous reasons for spirits to communicate and/or attach themselves to human beings. Readers interested in this subject must refer to A. Kardec. It is not possible lo elaborate here the complicated system of spiritual development of, and reason for, *causas.*

After the patient has been identified, the president describes his *causa* and may also state what type of spirit has come to the *centro* with the patient or tormented one.

The president explains how he was able to recognize the tormented one in the audience: "My spiritual guide allowed me to see a spirit that came with you, Juan. That spirit came through the *centro`s* front door. He stood in the door for a while before proceeding to the interior of this room." The president proceeds: "My *guia* cautioned me as to the intent of the spirit. At this time there is a consultation between members of the *cuadro espiritual* and the main protector or spiritual guide to the president. The spirit is allowed to proceed on his mission. The president informs the audience that the spirit went around the table, behind each medium, and turned to the audience. There, he found the person he came after, the patient. "That spirit," says the president, "stood behind you for a few minutes and, laughing loudly, it began to run around you. At the same time, I felt you were getting angry and uptight, and wanted to start a fight." This verbalization by the president, the patient denies or confirms. These feelings are not limited in time and place, and the president may put it in present or past, or may say that it will happen in a near future. The president continues: "After the spirit went around you a few times, it came to the table and placed that package which lies there." Usually, only the president sees the package; but his aides may say they also see the package. The patient, or subject, gazes at the table, anxious to know what is in the package. The curiosity of everybody at the *centro* is aroused. There is complete silence; you can practically hear the heartbeat of the person sitting next to you. The president may or may not reveal the contents of the package. The anxiety level has greatly increased.

Withholding the package's secret may increase not only the anxiety level but also the group's participation. The group now feels more stimulated to pray and ask or request the spirits to reveal the contents of the package. The president breaks the period of silence and says: "My spiritual guide showed me the package. As I tell you the contents of the package, I want you to follow me in a prayer for this spirit. I want you to cooperate and to report all you see about the patient. I want complete control of thoughts. Your mind must be now in communion with God and our redeemer Jesus Christ, because the package contains ... a knife." Immediately following, a medium stands up and bangs on the table. This is followed by a prayer. The medium, still giving signs that she/he was struck by vibrations from the spirit, remains in the chair with her hands tightly clasped on the table. Then the president requests every medium around the table to look at the patient and report his findings. Everyone about the table (therapy aides) is supposed to be working with only one patient, or tormented person. Another medium, reporting her findings, says: "While the president was revealing the contents of the package, I saw a coffin on the table." This might be followed by a description of the spirit that placed the coffin on the table. Another medium, following the president's directive to report on the subject (tormented one), adds that she saw stains of blood on the table and that she/he saw the subject involved in a fight. The picture now seems more complete. There are *evidencias,* reports of a knife, bloodstains, and a fight attributed to the subject and presumably brought in by a spirit. A fourth medium reports that she felt a sensation of extreme anger with the intention of striking at anyone. This statement may again prompt the direct intervention of the president. A full interrogation of the tormented one by the mediums on feelings and thoughts follows. Feelings and thoughts are to be confirmed or denied by the subject. If there is a denial on the part of the subject, the president may give a different interpretation to a feeling and allow the subject to elaborate on it. In any case, in this type of approach, the subject remains the central figure of attention. All comments, remarks, and interpretations are directed to the tormented one, and all mediums around the table are to concentrate on him. Mediums are to dismiss any vibrations from spirits other than those related to the subject under interrogation. They pride themselves on having this special talent to distinguish the different spirits. After the mediums have run out of *evidencias,* the spirit who caused the problem will speak through one of the mediums. This spirit will explain why he has troubled the subject and what he wants from him. The spirit would indicate that he is a spirit of *existencias pasadas,* or previous or past reincarnation. The spirit may have had a close relationship with the subject, i.e., in marriage or as a sibling, parent, neighbor, lover, etc., and wants a specific favor from the subject. According to Kardec's *espiritismo,* although there are many reasons for a spirit's communications and *causas,* mediums often find reasons of their own, besides Kardec's. Anyhow, they only do what other professions do —"advance their theories."

The spirit may be willing to leave peacefully without any further "work" from other mediums. Generally, this is followed by a prayer. The subject is given a thorough *despojo* and advised by the president concerning his problems and solutions. This experience may further convince the subject in *espiritismo.*

The first spiritual communication resembles that of a psychodrama session. The possessed medium as well as the tormented person share, on an equal basis, the attention of the audience. Both project their feelings on neutral grounds. Auxiliary egos could be used on both patient and medium. Through projection, externalization, and bodily physical movement, the medium benefits as much as the tormented one. Each one's problems and failures are blamed on an external force beyond their power and comprehension. Emotional parts of conflicting internalized objects, i.e., father, mother, grandparents, siblings, teacher, husband, wife, or children can be attributed to a spirit, and brings great relief. There is action by both subject and medium.

At the second spiritual manifestation, the subject or patient is a rather passive recipient of interpretations and interrogations by the president and mediums. The subject is the central focus of attention. There is a great feeling of expectation and suspense. The president plays a dominant role toward the mediums. No medium takes it upon herself/ himself to "work" the subject's *causa.* There seems to be an even contribution and share of feelings among mediums.

The intensity of the catharsis experienced by both subject and medium in the first case is hardly seen in the second. In the first presentation, the "possessed medium" keeps her pitch on the subject throughout the entire spiritual communication. The physical expression and verbalization of feelings in the first presentation is much more intense and tends to generate more involvement from the audience by identification. In the second case, there seems to be less acting out of feelings. There is no warmup period as in the first, and the president and the mediums make clear that their observations, interpretations, visions, etc., refer to the person standing in front of the table.

In the second presentation, there seems to be one patient and a leader with a group of co-therapists. The therapist's intervention is mostly through interpretation followed by the therapist's or the president's advice and remedies. Prayers and readings from Kardec and the Bible are a must in both cases. There are many other similarities and differences which the writer cannot examine here.

As indicated earlier, mediumship practice differs from medium to medium. This is further complicated by the level of development of both spirit and medium. If it is a low-level and sinful *atrasado* spirit, the manifestation will be very emotional. If it is a highly developed spirit communicating through a learned and educated medium, the mediumship experience would be different. The spirit of the Greek philosopher Socrates is expected to communicate differently from a spirit of an American tribal Indian. Spiritual communication will take as many forms as there are cultures, countries, and its effectiveness depends on the spiritual development of mediums and spirits.

It would be impossible for the writer to give an account of all spiritual manifestations that he has seen at the *centros*. Attempt has been made to present those cases or modalities of spirit communication that resemble either individual or group psychotherapy. However, it must be stressed that neither *centros* nor mediums claim to practice the above-mentioned therapeutic modalities.

Espiritismo, according to its members, is the true religion of primitive Christians. After the ascension of Jesus Christ, the apostles received the Holy Spirit. The Roman centurion and his household while talking to Peter received the Holy Spirit.

Similarly, *espiritistas* claim that non-holy spirits exist as well. They point out emphatically Jesus' command to his twelve disciples "to heal the sick, cleanse the lepers, raise the dead" (Matt. 10:18). In this command, *espiritistas* quote Jesus giving his disciples "power against unclean spirits, to cast them out" (Matt. 10:1). The Lord Jesus Christ told his disciples that power came through prayer and fasting. Fasting is not too common among *espiritistas,* but prayer is a daily must for all of them. Mediums find in the New Testament a wealth of material to reinforce and justify their belief in the world of spirits. Their most frequent quotations are "Thou dumb and deaf spirit, I charge thee, come out of him, and enter no more into him" (Mark 9:25); "and they cast out many devils, and anointed with oil many that were sick, and healed them" (Mark 6:13). Of course most mediums like to cite Luke 8:29, about the possessed of Gadarenes who begs Jesus to torment him no more. "For he had commanded the unclean spirit to come out of the man. . . . ."

Now let's turn to another *centro* whose president holds spiritual sessions slightly different from those in the previously mentioned case presentations.

As in most cases, the seance is begun with readings from Kardec's book, the gospel according to *espiritismo*. This book contains spiritual communications from well-known historical personages: Saint Augustine, John the Evangelist, Paul the Apostle, Pascal, Lazarus, and many others.
The readings are usually done by persons who are *desarrollando facultades,* developing spiritual faculties, to further train them in the *espiritismo* doctrine.

The person reads a paragraph or two aloud, and the president gives an interpretation which may or may not be shared by mediums around the table. It is not uncommon for mediums to offer interpretations which differ among themselves but are not too far off from that of the president. Often, persons developing *facultades* and members of the audience are welcomed to contribute to the interpretations. However, their comments and interpretations are carefully scrutinized and clarified by the mediums. It is a kind of supervision. When arguments arise as to the best interpretation, the president reinforces his point of view by citing other cases that have come to the *centro*. Thus, the president brings the issue from an intellectual debate to a here-and-now experience.

The president may recall a spirit communication at which time a person was told of a possible death in the family or of an embarrassing situation involving jailing, etc. Supporting the president or a favorite medium, a member in the audience may relate her/his experience while visiting the *centro*. He/she would say that his health has greatly improved since he began to come for spiritual workups. Allowing members from all levels of spiritual development as well as the audience to join in the interpretations promotes and stimulates individual participation, and more group interaction begins to take place. It is not limited to those around the table only. Theoretical discussion is also brought back to the table by recognition of a vision. The vision may have been seen by the president or the mediums, thus stimulating further interest in the discussion. Regardless of who saw the vision first, the president calls upon everyone in the *centro* to look inward in meditation and try to see the object in the vision. Members of the audience, as well as mediums, are requested to concentrate their thoughts and to see the vision mentally. From the second case of spirit communication, you will recall that a vision on the table was a package with a knife inside. In that case, the knife was the object in the vision. Members are encouraged to speak their minds and not to refrain or inhibit themselves, as it would only hinder or block spiritual development.

It is claimed that if one does not verbalize a spirit's vibration or vision, one would discourage the spirit, so that he may not want to communicate with that person again. This encouragement often provides for full participation from everybody in the *centro*. Individual members begin to ventilate or, rather, express their feelings and thoughts. The words "vision" and *evidencia* are interchangeable in *espiritismo* language in New York City. *Evidencia,* or evidence, means "proof." *Vidente* means a "seer" or "prophet," but also seeing. So, *evidencia* comes to mean both: "seeing a proof." As *evidencias* and visions begin to gain momentum in the *centro,* a genuine and productive group feeling takes place. It involves a large number of people and provides a sense of satisfaction and accomplishment. Members of the audience and those *desarrollando facultades* can relate directly to the mediums. This allows for the president or therapist to be shared by others.

Most often, the patient comes to the *centro* with the fantasy of having the therapist all to himself. Having his fantasy frustrated, the subject turns to a medium, thus partially replacing the president, and internalized conflict objects of the subject may be played out during the seance. In some instances, mediums and members of the audience sometimes compete for the *centro's* floor. As expected, the president restores order, and he goes around the table asking for more visions. This control of the audience by the president is further reinforced by his request for prayers after *evidencias* and visions are exchanged.

Interpretations by the audience and the mediums come after the working of *causas* or problems. The techniques used by the president during the last spirit communication are the following:

Readings from Kardec's book:
 Interpretations by:
 President
 Mediums—fully developed
 Mediums—not fully developed
 Audience
Citing or recounting previous cases in the *centro* by the president.
 Individual members past experience at the *centro.*
 Evidencias or visions by:
 President
 Mediums—fully developed
 Mediums—not fully developed
 Audience
 Working on *causas:*
 Medium to patient
 Patient's *despojo*
 Home remedies
 Prayers: They are said all along during the session, when requested by the president.

The readings are supposed to bring everyone's mind into unison. Mediums as well as the audience are to forget about the day's problems and worries and place their life and future in the hands of the Lord, Jesus Christ. It is a time of worship, and nothing but the spirit of God should occupy your mind. No talking or whispering of any kind is allowed during this time. No evil or sinful thought is to come to your mind. No feelings of jealousy, envy, or hate are to find access at the *centro* at this time. This most solemn period of worship is dedicated to God, so He can allow good spirits to come and bring a message of peace and supreme goodness to all. This is, in essence, the cleansing of the mind of harmful thoughts so that spirits can "see" the light and come to communicate with the living ones.

During interpretations they not only learn about the Gospel, but individual participation is promoted. Contributions by individual members give each one a sense of accomplishment and develop in each person a feeling of belonging to a group. Besides an intellectual exercise, interpretations provide for verbalization and projection of one's own feelings, thoughts, and experiences. The satisfaction gained through interpretations is an incentive for those who want further understanding and to progress in the *espiritismo* doctrine. Kardec's *Book of Mediums* elaborates on biblical passages given through the spirits of great saints and philosophers throughout history. It encourages reading the works of illustrious people who have dealt with life after death.

Evidencias reinforce group feelings and elevate the individual member to "person in process of developing spiritual faculties." They are seen as people on their way to mediumship, thus becoming status symbols. When *evidencias,* or visions, are confirmed by the president or fully developed mediums, it is a tacit recognition of mediumship and there is an open-door invitation to continue to come to the *centro.*

Often, visions are modified or otherwise changed by mediums. This might be an indication that the person needs further refinement and perfection of the senses to be able to pick up spiritual messages and vibrations. *Espiritismo* claims that every person is a potential medium, that mediumship is a God-given gift to all His children. However, they contend that some individuals are more sensitive and predisposed to spiritual communication than others. In the same manner that enlightened and highly developed spirits of the world beyond come to teach us, mediums have the responsibility of helping others develop their *facultades*. It is every *espiritista*'s best wish to be able to work out *causas* or problems for tormented persons. To be able to do unto others as it is done to him. It is a doctrine of works, not of faith alone. Mediums often spend three or four hours, three days a week, helping others with *causas*. "Deeds, not words," is the theme among *espiritistas*. They frequently quote St. Jame's Epistle, particularly 2:26: "For as the body without the spirit is dead, so faith without works is dead also."

Amalia Domingo Soler in her book, *Espiritismo,* writes: "To worship God, we believe, there is no need for temples or ministers, since God's best altar would be the heart of a virtuous man. . . . We shall worship Him in faith and in the practice of the supreme goodness."[5]

Working the *causas* brings medium and subject together in a very close relationship. It is not only a mutual exchange of feelings and thoughts, but physical contact as well. This is particularly evident during the *despojo* period. The medium goes around the subject's body and symbolically (for them it is reality) uses her hands to "take away" spiritual vibrations which are harmful to the subject. The effectiveness of the treatment is further strengthened by holding each other's hands and moving them up and around their heads. This circular movement begins slowly, but as the spirit is about to leave both medium and subject, it gains speed. When the spirit has left, both persons are exhausted from good physical exercise and release of tension. They seem to have helped each other. The medium practiced her religion not by faith alone, but by deeds. She worked out a problem for someone who was in need. She/he obeyed the Lord's command. In any event, whether the subject or patient recovers his/her health or his/her problems are solved, the medium has made this her/his main concern; and, the subject feels there is someone who is concerned about him/her. He will be looking forward to another *despojo* with the same medium.

After the *despojo,* it come the home remedies, supposedly dictated by the possessed medium's spirit. Remedies are multiple in kind and often seem so irrelevant and remote to the problem or *causa* that it really takes one who believes in supernatural powers to pay heed to them. G. M. Carstairs, in *Trunscultural Psychiatry* writes about healers' remedies in a village in northern India. "It became plain that the great majority of remedies which I saw deployed were physiologically speaking, quite irrelevant to the disease process itself. Instead, they were designed to bolster the morale of the patient and his family, and their effectiveness depended upon the authority and conviction which they were imparted".

It seems that in both cases, the Hindu and the Puerto Rican remedies effectiveness relied not so much on their relevance to the physical illness as on their power of suggestion. And suggestion imparted with authority, reinforced by the "magical power" attributed to mediums and spirits, often works wonders. In Puerto Rico, home remedies among rural dwellers are highly praised. Remedies for different illnesses are passed from one generation to another. It is still common for country people to have a sort of a botanical garden along with flowers for every disease. In the garden they plant and cultivate herbs and seeds which tradition has taught them have medicinal value. It is to be expected that the first treatment of the patient takes place at home with remedies from elders and the herbs from the garden. There is always a time during the day to use the remedies and a specific way of applying them that insiders know best. If home remedies, often followed by prayers, fail to bring improvement in the patient's health, it is time for him/she to see a physician. It is not uncommon to see a patient taking both treatments at the same time. Taking home remedies along with those of a physician may be done with the purpose of helping the patient as well as the effectiveness of the physician treatment. The elders or family members may feel that the physician, though well versed and knowledgeable in modern but foreign medicine, does not know the idiosyncrasies of country people. While they may feel that a medical doctor's treatment is good for the city person, it may not be for the rural dweller. If the physician prescribes medicine which is considered to have an adverse reaction in the patient, home remedies may also be given at the same time. For example, common colds which are to be treated by hot remedies would be carefully watched and evaluated if treated differently by a physician. If a cold-treatment regimen or medicine is included in the treatment of colds, it would create confusion and suspicion in the patient and his family, "since this violates the patient's conception of proper treatment."[7]

This practice is followed in New York City as well as on the island. In New York City, the *botanica,* or herb store, replaces the home garden on the island. When both home remedies and medical treatment fail to bring back the patient's health, his illness is said to be the work of bad spirits or *hechizos,* or witchcraft. As Helena Padilla, in her book *Up from Puerto Rico* says, "Physicians cannot cure super- naturally caused illness, rather, this is a job for Espiritistas or spiritualists."»

So we have home remedies, professional medical treat-ment, and the works of an *espiritista.* As indicated earlier, the *espiritista* also resorts to home remedies. However, unlike home remedies from the elders which were passed from generation to generation, the *espiritista* remedies are presumably dictated by a "spirit." And, one does not question the wisdom of a spirit. One wonders why this practice of home remedies and *espiritismo* treatment still exists in Puerto Rico and in New York City with all its "modern medical facilities." The writer's observations have led him to believe that, while the Puerto Rican relies more and more upon the medical doctor for his physical illnesses, it is not so with psychiatric problems. *Espiritismo* continues to attract many persons with emotional problems, often, if not competing with psychiatric clinics, existing side by side with them. The psychiatrist Ari Kiev says that *curanderismo* among Mexican-American in the Southwest persists because it works.'

We may make the same observation about *espiritismo* among Puerto Ricans. This statement may be partially supported by a survey undertaken by the writer when researching for this book about *Espiritismo* among Puerto Ricans in New York City.

Its findings will be discussed later on in the book.

Now, I would like to turn to another mediumship practice among *espiritismo* in New York City. It has received the writer's attention and concern because of its elaborate ritualism and often frightening fireplay. As a matter of fact, it is called working a spiritual *causa* with fire, *trabajando causas espirituales con juego.* The use of fire as a purifier and cleanser of our sins and imperfections has its origin far back in history. There is hardly any culture which has not viewed fire as some mysterious element. Moses' Ten Commandments were written with fire. Regarding Jesus, John the Baptist says: "He shall baptize you with the Holy Spirit and with fire."[10]

Accordingly, some mediums strangely believe in a "fire-bath" in order to prepare themselves for spiritual communication. Usually, a few drops of alcohol are placed in a pot and lit. Touching the fire with the fingers, the person symbolically cleanses his hands, arms, legs, and head with fire. As the medium dips her/his fingers in the pot of fire, she/he moves her hands around her head and body. This ritual is supposed to cleanse her of *impurezas,* or impurities, coming from the ground.

Earthly bad influences are destroyed by fire, and the person is then in a better position to receive spiritual contact and communications from spirits of the world beyond. The number of mediums working with fire seems to be small. Many *centros* do not allow this practice, and those which permit it have strict rules and regulations on its use. Although the number of mediums interviewed using fire as a cleanser is too small to make a significant statement about them here, there were more men than women. Male mediums seemed to show a greater ability to perform with fire than female mediums. For women, cleansing with fire is a difficult task. Their hair may be set on fire as they circle their hands around their head. Their clothing may also present another problem. On the other hand, men's hair is short (no long hair is found in *centros),* and consequently, there is less danger to exposure to fire. Men's short-sleeved shirts and pants that can be rolled up, places him in the more favorable position than women to work *causas* with fire. One wonders whether male mediums use fire as another way of male chauvinism. It may be another way for men to keep a superior feeling over women, as they do when performing an acrobatic feat.

Working with fire per se doesn't seem to add any additional power to the medium except his impressive ability to handle flames in front of an audience. The writer failed to see any other meaning except as a *despojo.* However, the elaborate, complex, and often dangerous handling of fire certainly impresses the subjects.

Along with fire there is another mediumship practice which makes a good impression on many *espiritistas.* After the prayers have been said, the medium is blindfolded with a large blue, yellow, or red handkerchief. Without either eye-to- eye or hand contact, with the patient or subject, the medium speaks out loud giving the patient's symptoms or *causas.* She either calls the subject by name or points out her finger in the direction of the subject supposedly having the mentioned symptoms. The subject is to affirm or negate the symptoms. There is hardly any physical contact between subject and medium. If there is any *despojo* or workout to be done, it is done by an auxiliary person, such as another medium sitting around the table. Blindfolding is practiced by both males and females. It tends to make a good impression on the audience also. In interviews with blindfolded mediums, they have stated that it helps them concentrate. They feel that the handkerchief around their eyes takes away external stimuli and distractions.

When questioned whether the handkerchief had any relationship to the spirit, most answered in the negative. The mediums interviewed felt that blindfolding would give them a feeling of preparedness, physically and mentally, for spiritual vibrations to come into their bodies. It seems to me that blindfolding not only eliminated external stimuli such as light from candles and eye contact with mediums and audience, but it really helped them get their thoughts together. We must bear in mind that before the session begins, mediums are talking about their problems, psychic experiences with others, and their own "visions." This overenthusiasm of their own work may be carried over to those at the table.

Thus, having a handkerchief around his head might well is like a pendulum to the hypnotist. The mediums direct their thoughts on the kerchief and away from their daily problems and thoughts. Instead of a hypnotic pendulum, a medium uses a handkerchief around his head. The writer would like to point out that schools of the occult, present and past, emphasize the use of objects—lit candles, circles, triangles, etc.—to initiate or facilitate concentration. The writer wonders if the use of Rosary beads is not another device used by Christians for concentration and meditation. While the writer can see some value in blindfolding as it relates to relaxation, meditation, and religious experience, fire-work by mediums didn't strike him as therapeutic. However, he recognizes his bias and is aware of his limitations. The mediums look at such devices as tools for inducing religious experiences, which are a subjective and personal feeling, while the writer's concern is practical reality.

The writer has tried to give an account of his observations at an *espiritista centro* and their comparison to individual and group therapy sessions. As stated earlier, he was very much impressed with the *espiritista* practice as it resembles psychodrama. Many conflicting parts of the person's or subject's ego could be seen at play. He felt that mediums were highly skillful and had a great understanding of people's problems. Mediums as well as subjects benefited from this approach. Equally important was the modality used when different subjects in the audience as well as mediums expressed their feelings freely. The approach is very similar to that in group sessions where the leader is a facilitator, but also has a good control over the group. There were also sessions when the patient was subjected to an intense interrogation by a group of mediums as well as by the president. This type of approach reminded the writer of enoucnter group sessions. However, the writer must point out that what was most common among the *espiritista centros* that he visited was that the patient was a rather passive subject. His role was to answer yes or no; except when he became possessed by a spirit and began to talk about his symptoms, or *causas.* This was often followed by bodily movements. The writer emphasized three modalities or approaches in an *espiritista* session because he could associate them with his own experiences and exposures to groups. However, he cannot say that two sessions were exactly the same in each modality; neither mediums nor subjects repeated themselves in each session. What he wants to say is that many experiences and problems were approached differently. But, for simplicity and better understanding, he catalogued them according to his exposure to group modality. Before the writer shows you a case demonstration, he would like to tell you about another "curiosity." Although every medium has her own personal *guia,* or spiritual guide (he took note of every *guia's* nationality or supposed nationality), over 90 percent claimed to be spirits of either Arab, Hindu, Indian, or African ancestry. The spirit identifies himself/ herself or the medium describes the clothing and other physical attributes of a given nationality. Arab spirits are known for their wisdom, Indian spirits for their high spiritual level, and African spirits for their magical power. Among Puerto Rican and Cuban mediums, African and Indian spirits were predominant.

Notes

' Raymond F. Marina et al., "Three Basic Themes in Mexican & Puerto Rican Family Values," *Journal of Social Psychology.* 48, (1958), p. 168.

'Samuel Z. Klausner, in *Psychiatry <8 Religion* (Garden City: The Free Press of Glencoe, 1964; London: Collier-MacMillan Limited. 1971), p. 116.

!J. L. Moreno, "Psychodrama & Group Psychotherapy," in *Sensitivity Training & Group Encounter* (New York: Grosset& Dunlap, 1971), p. 105.

* Elena Padilla, *Up from Puerto Rico.* (New York: Columbia Univ. Press, 1958) d 283.'Amalia Domingo Soler, *El Espiritismo* (Editorial Kier: Buenos Aires, 1 965), p. 23. *G. M. Carstaire,

"Cultural Elements in the Response to Treatment." in *Transcultural Psychiatry* (Boston: Little Brown & Company. 1965), p. 170.
'Alan Harwood, The Hot-Cold Theory of Disease; Implications for Treatment of Puerto Rican Patients."*M.A.* (May 17, 1971), p. 1153.
'Elena Padilla, *Up from Puerto Rico.* p. 283.

CHAPTER VIII

Ari Kiev. *Curanderismo: Mexican-American Folk Psychiatry* (New York: The Free Press. 1968), p. 6 ' "Luke 3:16.Case Presentation

The following is a case presentation of a twenty-eight-year-old female twice admitted to Kings County Hospital for a few weeks at a time. She later began going to *espiritista centros,* attending steadily for three years. She claimed not only that she has been out of the hospital and off medication, but that her marital relationship greatly improved. Mrs. A. Rosado (a pseudonym) has come to feel that her role as a wife and mother has changed for the good. She said she learned to like and respect men and that the female sex is no longer something to be ashamed of.

Mrs. Rosado was the youngest of three children, two females and one male. At the time of her birth, her father was disappointed at the birth of another girl; he wanted a boy. He took her brother with him and left the mother with the two girls. Before Mrs. Rosado was seven years old, she learned from her mother why her father had left them. At around the same time, Mrs. Rosado's older sister went to live with an uncle. Her mother could hardly provide for them. She never remarried. Mrs. Rosado remembers her mother as an affectionate, loving, and sweet person, but also as a sad, lonely, and sickly one. As a child, Mrs. Rosado said she always wondered why her father preferred a boy and rejected her. She looked at boys with curiosity. She often fought them, although she was much interested in their play activities and games;and she felt girls' games were silly. Although Mrs. Rosado claimed she did not hate boys, she was very suspicious of them. Boys had their own games and their own groups and did not include girls, except on a few occasions. As an adolescent she wanted to organize girls against boys. Her mother did not urge her to hate men, but always reminded her that they are cruel, punishing, and selfish. Mrs. Rosado was thirteen years old at the time her mother died of a heart attack in Puerto Rico. Mrs. Rosado remained in bed with her mother for four hours after her death. After her mother was buried, Mrs. Rosado said she spent three weeks in a hospital. After release from the hospital, she went back to her mother's house and to the same bed. Neighbors as well as relatives wanted to take her home, but she refused, so at age thirteen, she was living alone, in the same house and in the same bed her mother had occupied and died in. During the first six months after her mother's death, Mrs. Rosado used to go to the cemetery during the evening after the gates were closed, to "talk to her mother." She used to take care of her grave and placed fresh flowers on it every night. She had to climb up a five-foot-high wall protected with barbed wire. On a rainy night around Christmas, when she was climbing the wall of the cemetery, she lost her footing and cut her left arm. She remembers those were days of anguish and despair that she could not be with her mother at night at her grave.

At age eighteen, Mrs. Rosado migrated to New York City and married shortly after her arrival here. However, her marriage did not last long, and she separated six months after the marriage. Following the separation, Mrs. Rosado felt extremely confused, lonely, and rejected. She could not elaborate on why she separated from her first husband, but said he was selfish and "besides, 1 did not know what I wanted." During the following five years Mrs. Rosado was "married" (common law) three times and twice committed to a state hospital. The writer followed her activities for thirteen months.

The first contact with Mrs. Rosado was while the writer was doing some research about *espiritismo*. The *centro* where he saw her for the first time had as president, a forty-years-old, versatile, warm, friendly, concerned, and intelligent married male Puerto Rican. His second most important faithful mediums were a married couple with many years of *espiritismo* practice. They were highly respected by mediums and audience alike. Like the president, they projected warmth, understanding, compassion, and love for others. The first night the writer saw Mrs. Rosado at the *centro,* she was told by this couple that she had a spirit who made her very unhappy and wanted to see her go *loca,* or crazy. She was also told by the couple's spirit that Mrs. Rosado had been a failure as a wife. Mrs. Rosado responded in the affirmative, saying she had been in a state hospital and had separated from three husbands.

Immediately, the writer suspected that the couple had some previous knowledge about Mrs. Rosado's past life or that, at least, they had made a very good guess about it. However, Mrs. Rosado impressed him as an intelligent, alert, and attractive young lady. He wondered why she had failed three times in her marital life. He was concerned about her hospitalizations and could not explain Mrs. Rosado's failures in life and marriage. She looked physically healthy, and she did not show any symptoms that could lead one to recognize mental problems. As was said earlier, she was not only youthful and attractive, but very feminine in her attire. The writer wrote down the date, the subject's name, and the medium's or spirit's comments on Mrs. Rosado. She was asked by the president to return to the *centro* as she had *"un espíritu endurecido,"* a hardened spirit to work out. During the following session, on a Friday evening, the writer sat in a corner of the *centro* keeping an eye on what was going on among the members. Mrs. Rosado came in and took a seat three chairs behind the medium's table. There were other ladies sitting around her, but she did not establish contact with them. When the couple who had seen her in the first session came in, they went over and greeted her. The husband shook hands with her, and his wife joined him in the conversations.

A few minutes later, the *centra's* president, who was talking with another person, came to Mrs. Rosado and said, "How are you tonight, Señora?" Mrs. Rosado smiled, but did not answer him. After a few minutes, the *centro's* president and the couple took seats around the table. It was 8:30 P.M. and the session was about to begin. After the readings and prayers were said, spiritual communications began to be manifested. One of the mediums seated around the center of the table made a remark regarding Mrs. Rosado which was followed up by the couple. A spirit, communicating through the couple, told Mrs. Rosado that she had a spirit of past existence which did not allow her to be happy with her marital partners. The spirit continued, saying that he tormented Mrs. Rosado since childhood. According to the spirit, Mrs. Rosado had rejected him as a lover in a past incarnation. So he was taking revenge placing in her way all types of obstacles so she did not feel attracted to men. She was told by the spirit that she often hated men, but that it came from a *causa* that was placed on her. Mrs. Rosado, who had been answering to the spirit in the affirmative, could take no more and broke into tears. Screaming loudly and flying into rage, she said she hated men because they were cruel. She accused not only her ex-husbands as being cruel and selfish but also her father. The president comforted her, saying it was not her fault that she hated men. He indicated to her that it was mainly the spirit's fault.

The spirit wanted her to be an unhappy lady who could not hold a marital partner. Mrs. Rosado was told by the president and the couple that she must continue to attend weekly sessions at the *centro*. She was promised that all her problems would be resolved as her belief in *espiritismo* progressed. After her *causa* was worked out, she was instructed to do more praying at home. Mrs. Rosado became a steady and faithful worshiper of *espiritismo*. The writer followed her attendance for over a year and learned that she often visited the *centro* twice a week. During that period of time she developed a close and warm relationship with the couple and the president. She was encouraged to develop her spiritual faculties by regular attendance at the *centro* and by study of *espiritismo* doctrines. She was encouraged to read the books of Allan Kardec and Saint Theresa of Avila. Apparently, she became a protege of the president and the couple. Either she was allowed to talk about her feelings and problems every Friday evening, or a medium worked out her *causa.* It was emphasized with great persuasion that her hostile feelings toward the opposite sex were the workings of a spirit; that she should be strong and not allow herself to be dominated by those evil influences. Every conflicting act of behavior, feeling, or thought was projected and blamed upon a bad spirit. Thirteen months after the writer first saw Mrs. Rosado, the *centro* closed. The president went back to Puerto Rico. Almost two years later, the writer met Mrs. Rosado again. She said she is happily married and has not needed psychiatric treatment for more than three years. She is a devout *espiritista.*

The problems of the human body and the mind are very complex. Individuals, like cultures, develop their own peculiarity in resolving their problems. Presumably, Mrs. Rosado found in *espiritismo* a solution to her problems. Psychiatry seemed to be too far removed, detached, and sophisticated for this lady. *Espiritsmo,* on the other hand, was very close to her. She was "told" her symptoms and what caused them. She was immediately relieved of guilt by projecting it outside herself onto invisible spirits. She was allowed to act out her behavior without condemnation. She was welcomed by mediums that helped her seven days a week. She found in *espiritismo* a way of life; she could pray, socialize, dine, and go out with people who showed concern. There was the magic of religion: through the mediums she could blame her problems on supernatural forces. Her ability to work out her *causa* would secure her a place in the world beyond, according to *Espiritismo.*

The *New York Times* carried an article on mediums among the Navajo Indians and stated that, where the white mediums failed, the Navajo Indian medicine men succeeded, especially in the area of psychotherapy.[1] Like *espiritismo,* the Indian medicine man used religion as the moving force to bring back the patient's health.

Dr. W. A. McGarey in a medical commentary on America's greatest medium, Edgar Cayce, described a "flow of energy in the body which is in the shape of a figure of eight."[2] This energy is different from biochemical or other physical reactions in the body. *Espiritismo* mediums and other psychics have seen this "vibrating" energy, often called the aura. Espiritismo claims that this energy surrounding the body is the link between man's physical body and his spirit. Some mediums claim to have the power to increase this flow of energy through the fast circular moving of their arms. Increasing the intensity of this energy, mediums contend, allows them to facilitate communication with spirits of the dead. Through the aura, the person's spirit is supposed to enter and leave the body. In reading Edgar Cayce on healing, one becomes amused by his emphasis at the flow of energy around the body and its relationship to good health. One is led to believe that when a person is ill he must redirect the flow of energy so as to revitalize the damaged organ in his body. Interesting to note here is the thousand-year-old Chinese medicinal practice of acupuncture. Its practice, like Edgar Cayce's healing techniques, is based on a flow of energy throughout the body. In both cases, good health is dependent upon the normal flow of this nonphysical vibration and stimulation to bodily organs and nerve centers.

NOTES

[1] *New York Times.* July 7, 1972, p. 33.
[2] Mary E. Carter and W. A. McGarey, M.D., "Edgar Cayce" in *Healing* (New York: Paperback Library, 1972), p. 41.

Chapter IX
Prayers and Herbs

You have observed that *espiritismo* practice relies strongly on prayers for mediumship communication and the removal of *causas*. Mediums as well as the audience are involved in prayers and meditations. The manner of praying at most *espiritismo centros* is as follows: "Our Father which art in heaven, hallowed be thy name. Thy Kingdom come. Thy will be done on earth, as it is in heaven. Give us this day our daily bread, and forgive us our debts, as we forgive our debtors, and lead us not into temptation, but deliver us from evil. Amen."

This is most often followed by a prayer to the Virgin Mary as in the Catholic tradition. Pictures of Mary and Christ are very conspicuous at every *centro*. The Virgin Mary is assumed to be the intermediary between the Lord and man. During His crucifixion, Jesus commended John to Mary. In all the sessions that the writer attended there were more women than men. The woman-to-woman relationship and rapport would justify the prominent statues of the Virgin Mary at the *centros*.

Prayers are said throughout the session and must be repeated at home by the subject. Often prayers are said to minor celestial beings such as saints and spirits of loved ones. Barbara, Lazarus, and Caridad del Cobre seem to take a disproportionately large amount of prayer among all the saints. Besides prayer, the medium, like the medical doctor, has at his disposal a wide range of auxiliary health medicaments: herbs, ointment, water, crosses, etc. Probably, primitive man's attempt to resolve his health problem was by prayer. Illness was thought to be only the work of evil. Man, a tiny creature in an immense world, felt helpless and unprotected. On the ground, he was subjected to all dangers from hostile surroundings. Wild animals, hungry and capable of devouring him at the first snatch, often moved into his cave. Man and beast fed on fruit and vegetables, often one chasing the other. There were volcanoes, earthquakes, storms, quicksand, floods, and a number of deadly plants all posing a threat to man's survival.

Looking at the sky, man was amazed by its clearness and serenity, but bewildered and frightened to death by the lightning of a thunder storm. Man felt caught, a victim of strange forces from both the earth and the heavens. On the ground, he saw the largest and most powerful animal kill and extend his domain over the weakest one. The weak ones ran, leaving behind their prey for the stronger ones. When the beast had eaten and satisfied himself, he left rather peacefully to rest. Primitive man felt that as it was on the ground so it was in the sky. Thunder and lightning were giants in the sky throwing punches at each other. What prompted man to pray to appease these invisible forces and monsters, both on the earth and in the sky, is anybody's guess. However, man must have soon learned more practical methods to recover health and cast out evil forces. As man chose fruits and vegetables which were good for him, he must also have learned about plants which helped him recover his strength and energy. He learned which plants, fruits, and herbs had medicinal qualities. He learned to recognize and select them for his use. Here was an opportunity for someone to develop the power of life and death over his fellow man.

The person who could recognize the therapeutic value of herbs would be a powerful man in the tribe. This might well be the origin of the medicine man that is well represented in many primitive cultures and tribes still existing today. Herbs still are a great part of the pharmacopoeia of countries like China and India. Garlic and lemon, widely used today for innumerable reasons, were known to Mediterranean people for hundreds of years. Garlic was used, among other things, to treat intestinal parasites. For those persons having digestive problems, garlic is supposed to reestablish a bacteria balance in the digestive tract. It is also assumed to be a tranquilizer. Kristine Nalfi, M.D., as quoted by Richard Lucas, says: "Garlic is good as a laxative, lowers high blood pressure, cures indigestion, disinfects the content of the stomach, neutralizes poison and kills putrefaction bacteria."[1] Garlic as a food condiment is an indispensable part of Mediterranean and Latin cuisine.

Lemon, another "wonder fruit," is so widely used today for medicinal and culinary purposes that a simple statement in this book would not do justice to this "fruit of the world." Acerola and guava, the richest natural sources of vitamin C, were greatly known to Caribbean Indians. Papaya, another wonder of nature, is also known for its enzymes. It is said that Columbus and the Spanish conquistadores were amazed by the Indians' ability to digest large amounts of meat followed by pineapples and papaya. Papaya, guava, lemon, garlic, and acerola occupy a large section in today's health food stores.

The study and classification of herbs among ancient people was taken very seriously. Much of it has been lost to today's ready-made laboratory products. Josephus, the Jewish historian of Christ's time, wrote about the Essenes, a religious sect at the time: "They studied very carefully certain writings on medicine which dealt with the secret properties of plants and minerals."[2]

The Essenes were a religious group who felt that through them the "light of the world, Jesus Christ," would come. Many students and scholars believe that Christ was a member of the Essenes. The findings of the Dead Sea Scrolls shed much light in this area. Like E*spiritismo,* this religious group depended heavily on prayer and meditation for spiritual growth. But they also felt the need to cure and take care of thebodily or physical problems. They were supposed to be the best *therapeutes* of biblical times. The origin of the Essenes is rather obscure, although some individuals attribute this founding to Samuel. However, their religious teachings and medicinal practices have much in common with other "therapeutic" schools in Egypt, Tibet, and Persia. Dr. H. Spencer Lewis, in his book about Jesus, gives an excellent illustration of the relationship of Jesus to the Essenes.[3]

He traces the origin of the Essenes to the great Egyptian school of "Mysteries." These schools of the occult emphasized prayers as well as herbs for their patient's physical illness. However, much has been lost of that ancient wealth of information on the practical medicinal properties and uses of herbs. The old Egyptians seem to have accumulated an unbelievable amount of knowledge on plants. Using means and methods not clearly known to us today, even with our great technology, the Egyptians discovered the "mystery" of using some herbs to preserve the bodies of their displayed mummies thousands of years old. Our sacred book, the Holy Bible, takes note of the Egyptian interest and study of herbs. The first book of Moses says: "A company of Ishmaelites came from Gilead with their camels bearing spicery, and balm and myrrh, going to carry it down to Egypt."[4] This millennial civilization had accumulated an unusual amount of knowledge from nature. Their herbalists, we may say, had discovered many secrets of Mother Nature. Once more, prayer and herbs, heaven and earth, and spirit and body, seem to have found in the Egyptian's mystery schools a fine combination or fusion.

One German Chemist, Dr. R. Willstatter, said: "All life energy comes from the sun."[5] As the sunlight strikes the leaf of a plant, it immediately sets in process a very complicated "miracle." The solar energy transforms lifeless molecules of gas and water into living tissues and energy. Plants seem to have this rather exclusive privilege. And animals, man included, feeds on, and are kept alive by them. Chlorophyll, that green chemical found in plants, is used by you every day as a disinfectant in your toothpaste. Of course, Dr. Willstatter's remark on sunlight as the source of life is an old one. The rebellious Pharaoh (Amenhotep IV) Akhnaten, the world's first idealist, over three thousand years ago worshiped a god reflected in the sun as the source of all life energy on earth.

Herbalism, as you probably know, has a long tradition behind it. Although in some countries it is still highly useful and respected, in others it is discredited and often ridiculed. In the Western world, religion and the priesthood occupied a unique position in society. With the advent of Christianity as an institutionalized religion, the herbalist became associated, in many instances, with black magic. The alchemists of medieval times, with their weird experiments, were often accused of practicing witchcraft and condemned to die at the stake. However, herbalism and religion are still very much alive and useful in *espiritismo* practice. The *espiritista* medium has at her/his disposal a long tradition and general belief in herbs as having curative or healing powers. Herbs, seeds, and roots from all over the world are known to her. She learns to recognize them by sight, taste, and smell. She/he recommends a precise quantity, and stresses that herbs must be well kept in a safe place and away from children's reach, like any other medicine. The patient or subject is to take the amount recommended at the time and place indicated and nothing more. These herbs, when taken, are to be followed by prayers. Unlike psychotherapy or institutionalized religion, *espiritismo* provides for the spirit and the body. Rather than relying upon abstract words and thoughts, *espiritismo* practice is reinforced by a practical, concrete, and realistic approach. The subject is given something tangible and material to hold on to—the herbs—while he waits for the next session. If prayers don't do anything for him, herbs will. The patient has still another alternative. If prayers and herbs do not give him satisfaction, he can continue to attend *espiritismo* sessions and allow mediums to work out his *causa.* He ventilates his problems in an atmosphere of acceptance and understanding. The support he receives from the *centro's* members gives him a sense of security and self-reliance. He finds people in the *centro* who talk about the same experiences he has had without fear of criticism or condemnation.

However, we must not forget that Puerto Ricans, whether *espiritistas* or not, have relied upon herbs for their health problems for centuries. The writer may add: so does the rest of the world as well. When the Spaniards began colonization of the island, they found Indians who worshiped idols and drank herbs to expel the evil spirits who had invaded their bodies and made them ill. Adding to this Indian tradition were the contributions of the Spanish colonist who brought with him to the island herbs and the limited medicinal practice at that time. The African slave also carried to the island his tribal medicinal practice. We may say, without fear of exaggeration, that *espiritismo* in Puerto Rico is the amalgamation of religious experience and primitive medicinal practice of Europe, Africa, and America. Although *botanical* or herb stores, and *espiritismo* sessions continue to flourish in New York City, one would never know whether they increase or decrease because of the secrecy surrounding them.

For many thousands of Puerto Ricans, *espiritismo* is still a hope, no matter how dim that hope might be. Many emotionally unstable people find a haven in *espiritismo* and continue to be productive members of society because of it. They hold jobs and take care of their families. As said earlier, *espiritismo* accepts them. One wonders whether our mental institutions do. Morton

Birnbaum, M.D. and lawyer, says: "The mentally ill are warehoused in hospitals, they are rejected by everyone."[7] He goes on to say that in a case he fought in court, there was one nurse and one doctor for 950 patients. It is often against these kinds of conditions that relatives prefer the homemade medicine of herbs and prayers. The New York State mental health commissioner, Alan Miller, in an interview for the *New York Sunday News,* on mental health care, said that until a decade ago when new tranquilizers were introduced, "big institutions (hospitals) were 'madhouses' partly as a result of what such facilities did to people."[8]

After you have read these two last public statements from reputable health professionals, you can not but conclude that *espiritismo* practice is in a good position to compete with institutionalized mental health care facilities.

Herbs and oils prescribed by mediums are purchased at the *botanica.* Herbs are arranged, weighed, and labeled in medicinelike fashion and are to be taken strictly as recommended at the *centro.* The *botanica,* besides selling herbs, oils, roots, and incense, carries all types of prayers. The front window is adorned with plaster figurines of Christ or the Virgin Mary, or with Indian heads. In New York, as in Puerto Rico, homes are adorned with pictures of Jesus and Mary.

Among the many herbs prescribed by mediums, I will name those most often used. The diagram, pages 80-81, there is a list of herbs describing the manner in which they are taken or used. It also describes their therapeutic effect according to *espiritismo* practice. In the left column is the name of the herb. The center column gives the manner in which the herb is to be taken. The right column represents its presumable therapeutic effects. There are many causative factors for the prescribed herbs. For the purpose of better understanding and to facilitate this study, the writer grouped the causative -factors into six main therapeutic purposes, namely: tranquilizer, body buildup, laxative, soothing drink, protection against evil spirits, and other. Under each of these headings are the reasons why the herbs are recommended. The headings are lettered A, B, C, D, E, and F.

Definitions of the therapeutic value of the herbs are also given.

How are Taken

	Drink	Eat	Bath	Spray	Rubbing compound	Placed under objects, chair, pillow, mattress
1.Almacigo	B					
2.Albahaca		E	F.			
3. Anamu		E	E			E
4. Anisette	D					
5.Artamiza		E	E			
6. Berbena		E				
7.Chinese Apple		F				
8.Cundiamor		B-F				
9. Garlic		A-E-F			E	E
10.Hedionda	A-C		E			
11.Lemon, Orange Juice	A-C-D-F					
12. Malva	A-C-F	B	E			
13.Marigold		F	E	E		
14. Mint	B	B	E			
15 Papaya	C	C				
16.Pumpkin Seeds		F-C-B				
17.Raisin Seeds		B-A				
18. Rose Hips	A		E			
19. Ruda	B		E			E
20. Savila	A-D					

78

21.Sesame Seeds   B   B
22. Snake Oil   F
23. Socato   D   D
24.Tartago Spurge   E   F
25. Yanten   A-B   E

Therapeutic Value:

A - Tranquilizer
b - Body Buildup
C - Laxative
D - Soothing drink
E - Protection against evil spirits
F - Others

A	B	C	D	E	F
Tranquilizer	Body Buildup	Laxative #	Soothing Drink	Protection Against Evil Spirits	Other
Nervousness	Physical weakness	Digestive system problems	Internal irritation	Spiritual *causa*	Arthritis
Heartburn	Tiredness	Constipation	Feeling hot or cold	Hair pulling	Sore throats
High Blood pressure	Dizziness	Indigestion	Feeling thirsty	Sees shadows	Tonsi Litis
Palpitations	Forgetfulness	Full stomach	Stomach gases	Hears voices of evil spirits	Parasites
Insomnia	Sadness	Gases		Feels very cold in the back	Diabetes
Restlessness	Boredom	Unable to eat certain foods		Goose pimples	Kidney and liver Complaint

79

Definition of the therapeutic value
Intuitional
messages
Feels body touched by the spirits
Visions
Pains
Headaches
Suicidal
Thoughts
Alcoholism
Drug
addiction
Vague
Fears

By placing a letter in each square, the writer tells you how the herb is used and for what purpose. Sometimes an herb may be used differently and for a different purpose as in garlic. It is used or recommended as a tranquilizer, as a protection against evil spirits, and against internal parasites. Accordingly, garlic is marked A-E and F. It is eaten, used as a rubbing compound and placed under household objects. You also have herbs like anamu, which is used differently (in the bath, sprayed, placed under household objects), but all for the same purpose: protection against evil spirits. So it is marked E in the columns of therapeutic effect.

You also have orange juice, which is taken as a tranquilizer, laxative, soothing drink, and other. For this reason, it is marked A, C, D, and P. The writer wants to point out that the uses or therapeutic effects of herbs here enumerated are not exhausted in the six categories. There were other effects which he did not bring out. The writer wrote only about those which were more frequently used at the *centros*. There were many more herbs recommended by mediums, but he chose the most popular ones. The causative factors or reasons for which the herbs were prescribed are enumerated as closely as explained by the subject. In presenting the chart, the writer does not attempt to approve or disapprove it. His sole purpose is to show you the value put on the herbs at the *centros* so that you might have a better understanding of *espiritismo* and its believers. He does not attempt to form conclusions or to make generalizations.

The medicinal and nutritious value of some of the herbs and fruits prescribed by mediums is unquestionable, although they may not be recommended as such. As an example you have papaya, garlic and lemon juice. They make up part of today's American pharmacopoeia. They also have high nutritional value. Health food stores carry large quantities of them. Malva is used in Puerto Rico and in Spain as a food and medicine. While some of the herbs and fruits prescribed by these mediums have excellent medicinal and nutritional value, others, marked E, a proportionately large number, are for external use only and as a religious device. They are recommended for the sole purpose of expelling bad spiritual fluids and influences. There are many ways of effecting behavioral changes in the individual to bring about better health and growth. From time immemorial, man has tried to probe his own mind, to know himself better. Meditation and herbs are known to be used by ancient people and still practiced today in many parts of the world. The foothold that hypnotism and psychoanalysis had in the past is declining. Dr. Skinner and Dr. Delgado (pioneers in behavior therapy), with their drastic and unorthodox methods of behavior modification, might well be showing the way to a world of "human robots." The use of prayer and herbs, the oldest form of the medical practice, is still very alive because it is very useful and helpful to many people, and, besides, it doesn't pose the threat of either Skinner or Delgado's dehumanizing methods.

Notes

Richard Lucas, *Nature's Medicines.* (New York: Award Books), p. 52.

Edward Schure, *The Light of the Mysteries: Jesus* (Blauvelt, New York: Rudolf Steiner Publications. 1971), p. 56.

Dr. H. Spencer Lewis, *The Mystical Life of Jesus* (San Jose, California: Gran Logia Suprema de Amorc, Departamento de

Publicaciones, 1967) Spanish Version. Gen. 37:25. King James Version.

As quoted by H.E. Krishner, M.D., in *Nature's Healing Grasses.* (California: H.C.

White Publications. 1972), p. 24.

Robert Silverberg, *Akhnaten. The Rebel Pharaoh* (Philadelphia and New York: Chilton Books, 1964).

M.D.   Fights for the Mentally ill, *New York Daily News.* April 30, 1973, p. 42. Mental Health Care: A New Diagnosis, *New York Sunday News.* April 8, 1973, p 131.

M.DI.

Chapter X
Research survey on psychiatric patients

The writer's curiosity about *espiritismo* among Puerto Ricans, both on the island and in New York City, led him to undertake this research, the purpose being to trace the origin, introduction, and development of this religious cult in Puerto Rican society. This was followed by the writer's active participation at *espiritismo centers* which have been described in the previous chapters.

Having partially satisfied that curiosity, the author would like to refer you to another part of the research survey. It is, rather, two parts divided into different sections. The first part deals with a hundred patients who were undergoing psychiatric treatment. The information was gathered through a questionnaire which consists of three pages. The first page contains identifying data about the patient. The second page deals with the presenting problems as described by the patient. The patient wrote a check mark describing each of his/her symptoms. This led to a tentative diagnosis of the person's problems. It also provided for the identification of problems other than psychological, i.e., marital, school, housing, and welfare problems. The third page deals with the patient's feelings, and an evaluation of the mental health practitioner, specifically the social worker. The rationale behind theselection of the social worker as the mental health practitioner, and not a psychiatrist or psychologist, is based on that the vast majority of the persons interviewed were treated by social workers.

Secondly, "talking therapy" among the poor in New York City is done almost entirely by social workers. Thirdly, the word *psychiatrist* among the Puerto Rican poor is "taboo." To go to a psychiatrist means to be "crazy," "mentally insane," *malo de la mente*.

In part one of this survey, the questionnaire is designed to elicit general information on the patients. It includes age, sex, religion, marital status, employment, weekly income, dwelling, education, place of birth, length of time in New York City, members of the patient's family living in Puerto Rico, and the number of individuals in the immediate family. The age item is divided in groups often from twenty up—20 to 29, 30 to 39, etc. The writer feels each ten-year group is representative of a certain emotional stability and social interest. The study showed that 36 percent of those going for psychiatric treatment were between thirty and thirty-nine years of age. Eighty percent were females of the Catholic faith and were unemployed. Sixty-three percent were married. Fifty percent were on welfare. Thirty-four percent had a total weekly income of $149. Either or both, the husband and the wife were employed at the time. Only two persons had a weekly income of over two hundred dollars. While 53 percent of those interviewed here came from the countryside in Puerto Rico, 87 percent came from other than the San Juan metropolitan area.

Interesting data which the author was not aware of prior to the survey concern the dwelling distribution among this group. There have been a lot of housing projects and cooperatives built where this group of Puerto Ricans lives in New York City. However, the study showed that nearly 70 percent live in apartment houses only three and four stories high. These are dilapidated, run-down, high-rental buildings, filled with roaches and rats. Heat and hot water are a luxury in these buildings rather than a necessity. One wonders whether this is another area where Puerto Ricans are pushed out of new living facilities in the city's housing projects and private cooperative houses.

In relation to education, the studied group showed that 50 percent of the patients had at least an eighty-grade education. Twelve percent out of that 50 had finished high school and 2 percent had gone to college.

Eighty-five percent had relatives of the immediate family still residing in Puerto Rico; consequently they were their parents, brothers, sisters, and children. Sixty percent had lived thirteen years or more in New York City, while 18 percent had lived less than two years in the city. In 23 percent of the cases studied there were three members in the family makeup; 22 percent had five members; 18 percent, four members; and 17 percent, two members. The remainder was distributed between one and ten members in the family constellation.

Many observations can be made from the above-mentioned data. Salient features are the sex and religion variables. As said earlier, 80 percent were female Catholics. My personal experiences and observations only add to this finding. It is the female, the Puerto Rican mother, who goes for psychiatric help. She is responsible for the care, discipline, and supervision of her children. She might feel responsible for securing help for herself so as to better provide for her family. The role of the Puerto Rican mother in New York City continues to change as she becomes a dominant figure in the family constellation. One must remember that 63 percent were married at the time of the survey, while 19 percent were separated. Eleven percent was divorcees and seven percent single.

Among the many questions coming to the author's mind one is: How does the Puerto Rican male cope with his psychiatric problems? He doesn't show up at psychiatric clinics. Are we correct to expect the percentage of males in need of psychiatric help to be equivalent to that of women? Does he give vent to his pent-up feelings and problems through other mechanisms? Families on welfare have been forced to say that the father is not at home to be eligible to receive economic assistance. The male, fearful of being reported to the welfare department with the result that his family loses its benefits, may decide not to go for help at the clinic, continuing to suffer and stay in the background.

Perhaps there are many other reasons which the reader could attribute to the problems exposed above, but the purpose here is to highlight the obvious ones. In the items or variables in which the author did not give a complete breakdown, it was felt that the remaining percentages were so minimal as to become irrelevant to the main points of the study.

However, a point of curiosity in reference to religion is that nine persons indicated that they were Catholic and *espiritista* at the same time. They felt there was no conflict of interest being both. Two persons stated their religion as *espiritismo*. They were quite emphatic about their belief and insisted that *espiritismo* was their only religion.

The second part of the survey enumerated the problems presented by the patient. The patient checked a list of symptoms which were conducive to a diagnostic impression. The list of symptoms was done under consultation with a psychiatrist. The first group of symptoms described a person with anxiety neurosis. The second group of symptoms was descriptive of a depressed person. Aaron T. Beck's Depression Inventory was used for this category. The third group of psychological problems was those of schizophrenia. The interviewer checked for hallucinations, delusions, persecutory ideation, disoriented to place and time, affect, thought content, reality contact, loose association, and other observable symptoms of the illness.

This breakdown in symptomatology was done with the intent to avoid confusion and misinterpretation of information about the patient studied. Among many Puerto Ricans, particularly believers in *espiritismo,* claims are made that they see and talk to an *espíritu,* or ghost. This might be wrongly interpreted by the unaware and untrained therapist.

The rest of the page deals with other social and concrete

problems. Salient among them were welfare and housing problems. Marital discord and children's school problems came in second. Economic insecurity permeated all other problems. According to the responses, 33 percent would have been diagnosed as having "anxiety neuroses." Eleven percent would be seen as suffering from depression, and 10 percent as schizophrenics. The fourth group, those with marked anxiety compounded by economic and school-children problems, was 13 percent. Two percent of this group was in the depressed category.

Fourteen percent stated that their problems were solely economic. They were unskilled, unemployed, and with a very limited education. Ten percent of those interviewed felt they had a problem with the school system. They showed no severe signs of undue anxiety about this, they just believed that the schools were not doing enough for their troubled children, and they felt somewhat helpless.

It is interesting to note that only 2 percent of the patients came for help with marital problems. The remaining 5 percent, that checked "other," came for nursing-home placement, maternity, abortion, adoption, and contraceptive information. However, 78 percent of the responses stated that the patients had either seen shadows or heard voices at least once during the last five years.

As you remember from previous chapters, *espiritistas* claim to see shadows and hear voices of spirits even in the initial stage of mediumship development.

The last part of the questionnaire deals with individual responses to *espiritismo* and the psychotherapist (social worker). The patient wrote down how many times he had seen each one. Thirty-five percent stated they had never gone to an *espiritista* for their problems, while 23 percent had gone four times to a mental health clinic for treatment. A good number of persons among the 30 percent who had not seen an *espiritista* were willing to see one, but were afraid and suspicious. They attributed to the *espiritista* some kind of power they could not explain.

Seventeen percent had seen an *espiritista* for ten visits or more. Fourteen percent kept at least ten appointments with the psychotherapist. Twenty percent went to a mental health clinic only once, while 15 percent went twice.

Thirteen percent saw the *espiritista* four times, while another 13 percent saw him once. Almost twice as many people kept four appoinoments with the psychotherapist as with the *espiritista.* Four appointments seem to be the average number of visits to the mental health clinic.

Ten percent saw the *espiritista* twice, and another 10 percent saw him three times. The remaining 2 percent saw him five times. The number of visits to the *espiritista* almost stopped after the fourth visit, except for 17 percent of the believers.

The psychotherapist, on the other hand, although his appointments sharply declined after the fourth visit, was able to maintain the interest of the remaining patients longer in treatment. Three percent kept five appointments; 7 percent kept six; and 9 percent kept eight appointments.

As stated earlier, 14 percent kept ten or more visits with the therapist. The research does not show whether this group was also receiving medication. Medication is seen as a "concrete service" different from "talking therapy." The patient tends to feel obligated to come for treatment so he can get medication.

With both, the E*spiritista* and the psychotherapist, there is a core group which remained faithful even after the tenth interview. Moreover, 65 percent saw the *espiritista* before or simultaneously with the psychotherapist.

There are a few remarks by the patients which might shed light on their feelings about psychiatric treatment which would be interesting to point out here. Some of the patients interviewed insisted that their illness was not mental but "nerves." They indicated that their "nerves were weak" and felt there was nothing wrong with their heads. This group of patients felt that "sickness of the head" was extremely difficult to cure and a disgrace to the family. However, if you had a "nerve illness" it could be treated with medication, preferably with vitamins. They stated they were taking vitamins, although their prescriptions showed differently.

Social worker mental health clinic	number of visits	Espiritista
	0	35
20	1	13
15	2	10
9	3	10
23	4	13
3	5	2
7	6	0
0	7	0
9	8	0
0	9	0
14	10 & over	17
100	Total	100

The following two statements, which are part of the questionnaire, elicited some of the patients' feelings toward E*spiritismo* and emotional problems. The patients were required to check their preference on a scale of five.

First statement

Espiritistas do not help people resolve their emotional problems. Forty-nine percent either agreed or agreed strongly, while 21 percent were uncertain. The remaining 30 percent disagreed or disagreed strongly.

Second statement

Most emotional problems are caused by spirits. Twenty-one percent either agreed or agreed strongly. Fourteen percent were uncertain. Sixty-five percent either disagreed or disagreed strongly with the statement.

QUESTION A		QUESTION B
16	DISAGREED STRONGLY	42
14	DISAGREED	23
21	UNCERTAIN	14
19	AGREED	14
30	AGREED STRONGLY	7
100	TOTAL	100

STATEMENT A
Espiritistas do not help people resolve their emotional problems.
STATEMENT B
Most emotional problems are caused by spirits.

In Statement A from the response of the group interviewed we read that 49 percent agreed with the statement that *espiritistas* do not help people resolve their emotional problems. Thirty percent disagreed with the statement, meaning that *espiritistas* do help people resolve their emotional problems. A significant number, 21 percent of those interviewed, were uncertain.

In Statement B, 65 percent disagreed that most emotional problems are caused by spirits. Twenty-one percent responded in the affirmative. Fourteen percent were uncertain.

CHAPTER XI
EPILOGUE

The Puerto Ricans—alienated, rejected, and pushed out of institutionalized services, i.e., schools, churches, hospitals, and other facilities were forced to form their own local "groups" and "churches" to survive in an unaccepting society. Unlike the European immigrant of past generations, the Puerto Rican adult did not form gangs to strike out at other groups as was so prominent in the nineteenth and early twentieth centuries. There are no murderous gangsters, cutthroats, or thieves of "reputation" among Puerto Ricans. They did not get involve in taking over the prostitution or gambling rackets. Joseph P. Fitzpatrick, in *Delinquency and the Puerto Rican,* writes: "the marvel is not that there has been so much delinquency (among Puerto Ricans) but that there has been so little."[1] One might argue that ethnic groups of past generations were only able to break into American society because of gang formation. They were thus able to have territorial, business, and political control of their neighborhoods, often using violence and crime to attain such control. These groups were able to express and externalize their anger and frustration. They demanded and got their "piece of the pie." So, gang formation gave them strength, self-confidence, and accomplishment. These personality buildups placed them in the forefront of American success.

On the other hand, the Puerto Rican with his history of colonialism remained a passive and submissive individual. Instead of forming groups for self-protection, he turned to religion for relief and comfort. But religion did not help him fight and conquer the outside world. It was only an escape from the hard reality of everyday life. Furthermore, the local church often created more guilt, thus creating a weaker individual. The church after the 1950s which proved to be helpful to the Puerto Rican-born adult was inadequate for the New York City-born adolescent of the 1960s. To the Puerto Rican adolescent, both the city and his own local group failed him. He turned to drugs, truancy, etc. The rate of drug addiction is said to be higher among them than among any other ethnic group in the city.

Unlike other groups, Puerto Ricans have internalized their anger and frustration, thus feeling incompetent and inadequate. Moods of apathy, resignation, and depression permeate their personalties. Shooting drugs, a self-destructive device, has taken the lives of many.

The New York City school system not only closed its doors to the Puerto Rican students, but further built the gap between them and the American society. The Puerto Rican parent had a dream. He dreamed he would have a decently paid job for himself and a good education for his children. For the Puerto Rican immigrant, New York City was thought of as a promised land in a "nation conceived in liberty, and dedicated to the proposition that all men are created equal." He was expecting "liberty and justice" for all. On the island, it was mandatory that he read Lincoln and memorize the Pledge of Allegiance to the Flag of the United States. However, naively, he did not understand the difference between the theory and the pragmatic realities of the American way of life.

Puerto Ricans, like previous immigrants, are dreamers. However, the Puerto Rican's dream turned out to be a nightmare. He has been denied the opportunity many others had—the opportunity to fulfill his dream. An American citizen by birth, the Puerto Rican has been pushed out in both New York City and on the island. On the island, as in New York City, the Puerto Rican child is enmeshed in a school system which is not geared to meet his complex and multiple needs. On the contrary, the system highlights and emphasizes his weaknesses, deficiencies, and failures. Insecure and unable to determine his political and economic future, the Puerto Rican on the island dreams that some day, through forces not his own, he will be a free and independent individual. One wonders if *espiritismo* is not one of the binding forces which would thrust the Puerto Rican forward to achieve his dreams. This analysis and depiction of Puerto Rican in New York City needs to be reviewed to show our accomplishment despite multiple obstacles. Honorable Supreme Court Judge Sonia Sotomayor was raised in The Bronx, New York City. There are three Puerto Ricans in Congress who must have overcome problems as depicted in our study. There are many Puerto Rican professionals like medical doctors, lawyers, pharmacists, teachers, scientists, bankers, and more, who have overcome all challenges and remained truthful to their identity while they accomplished the American dream. We were loyal subjects to Spain, and we are successful American citizens. We have defended our system of government as Admirals, Generals, Captains as well as thousands of regular soldiers during all

American wars during the XX century.

Notes

Rev. Joseph P. Fitzpatrick, "Delinquency and the Puerto Ricans," Lecture at Fordham University, October 8, 1959